SHAKESPEARE'S STRONG WOMEN

The wit, wisdom and wickedness of his fiercest female characters

ROYAL
SHAKESPEARE
COMPANY

HarperCollins*Publishers*

HarperCollins*Publishers*
1 London Bridge Street
London SE1 9GF

www.harpercollins.co.uk

HarperCollins*Publishers*
Macken House, 39/40 Mayor Street Upper
Dublin 1, D01 C9W8, Ireland

First published by HarperCollins*Publishers* 2026

10 9 8 7 6 5 4 3 2 1

Text © HarperCollins*Publishers* 2026
Material marked as contributed by RSCE © Royal Shakespeare Company 2026
Character illustrations by Clementine Hope © HarperCollins*Publishers* 2026

Liz Marvin asserts the moral right to be identified as the author of this work

A catalogue record of this book is available from the British Library

ISBN 978-0-00-880940-9

Printed and bound in the UK using 100% renewable electricity at CPI Group (UK) Ltd

All rights reserved. No part of this publication may be reproduced, stored in a retrieval system, or transmitted, in any form or by any means, electronic, mechanical, photocopying, recording or otherwise, without the prior written permission of the publishers.

Without limiting the exclusive rights of any author, contributor or the publisher of this publication, any unauthorised use of this publication to train generative artificial intelligence (AI) technologies is expressly prohibited. HarperCollins also exercise their rights under Article 4(3) of the Digital Single Market Directive 2019/790 and expressly reserve this publication from the text and data mining exception.

TITANIA – *A Midsummer Night's Dream* 128

VOLUMNIA – *Coriolanus* 136

VIOLA – *Twelfth Night* 144

DESDEMONA – *Othello* 152

PAULINA – *The Winter's Tale* 160

PORTIA – *The Merchant of Venice* 170

TAMORA – *Titus Andronicus* 180

THE PRINCESS OF FRANCE – *Love's Labour's Lost* 188

INNOGEN – *Cymbeline* 196

MARGARET OF ANJOU – *Henry VI, Part 1;*
Henry VI, Part 2; Henry VI, Part 3 and Richard III 206

MIRANDA – *The Tempest* 214

CRESSIDA – *Troilus and Cressida* 224

ISABELLA – *Measure for Measure* 234

JULIA AND SILVIA – *The Two Gentlemen of Verona* 244

KATHERINA (KATE) – *The Taming of the Shrew* 254

EMILIA – *Othello* 264

Acknowledgements 272

CONTENTS

FOREWORD *by Juliet Stevenson CBE* 5

PREFACE *by the Royal Shakespeare Company* 10

INTRODUCTION – *Backwards and in Heels* 15

LADY MACBETH – *Macbeth* 18

BEATRICE – *Much Ado About Nothing* 26

OPHELIA – *Hamlet* 34

HERMIA AND HELENA – *A Midsummer Night's Dream* 42

HELEN – *All's Well That Ends Well* 50

CLEOPATRA – *Antony and Cleopatra* 58

CORDELIA – *King Lear* 68

ADRIANA – *The Comedy of Errors* 76

ROSALIND – *As You Like It* 84

JULIET – *Romeo and Juliet* 92

OLIVIA – *Twelfth Night* 102

MISTRESS QUICKLY – *Henry IV, Part 1; Henry IV, Part 2; Henry V and The Merry Wives of Windsor* 110

GERTRUDE – *Hamlet* 120

FOREWORD

What studied torments, tyrant, hast for me?
What wheels? Racks? Fires? What flaying? Boiling?
In leads or oils? What old or newer torture
Must I receive, whose every word deserves
To taste of thy most worst? Thy tyranny,
Together working with thy jealousies –
Fancies too weak for boys, too green and idle
For girls of nine – O, think what they have done
And then run mad indeed, stark mad! For all
Thy bygone fooleries were but spices of it.

These were some of the first lines of Shakespeare that I ever spoke on stage. They belong to Paulina in *The Winter's Tale* (Act 3, Scene 2), the faithful servant-companion to Hermione, queen to Leontes, whom he has publicly and wrongfully accused of infidelity in an irrational fit of jealousy.

    It was early in my training at drama school, and it was the term in which we tackled Shakespeare for the first time. What a role to cut my teeth on: I was a skinny, shy 19-year-old with very limited life experience, and without much confidence in my own skills or aptitude for acting. Here was a character whose moral courage, fiery temper and passionate truth-telling had to be fully inhabited. It was a big stretch to find the breath to fill these words – to learn the technique that would do justice to the glorious alliteration, the stabbed syllables of her contempt, the driving rhythms of her speech. I doubt I pulled it off, but I do remember the sensation of yielding my tentative self to the might of that language. And the feeling was thrillingly empowering, as though it was not I who was embodying Paulina, but rather she who was embodying me, with all her maturity and force.

The following year I graduated, and soon found myself at the Royal Shakespeare Company. I started at the bottom, playing wordless bits and pieces in the opening productions of the season. But by a very lucky chance, I soon got upgraded and was given incredible opportunities to stretch my inexperienced wings. The first Shakespeare heroine I played there was Titania in *A Midsummer Night's Dream* in 1981. This glorious production by Ron Daniels saw the fairy world as one populated by forces of nature with power and anarchic sexual drive. After that, I enjoyed nine blissfully challenging years playing a range of Shakespeare's leading women, steeping myself in the exploration of them.

As each role arrived, I became aware of the weight of dramatic and literary tradition by which the character had been somewhat diminished. They appeared to have been pre-judged. In my third season, for example, I played Isabella in *Measure for Measure*, and in reading around the play I was shocked to discover that those traditions had her firmly caged in the cliché of 'frigid hysteric', because she refuses to have sex with Angelo when he bribes her with the pardon of her condemned brother. But, to my excitement, and in collaboration with the director Adrian Noble, we found the text did not support that view. Stepping into Isabella's shoes, filling her words with my breath, and allowing the pattern and pulse of her lines to lead the way, I found someone far removed from that misogynistic

FOREWORD

stereotype. By no means frigid, she is a woman of burning intellect, passion and wit. Even as she finds the nerve to challenge Angelo's authority, the words Shakespeare gives her lift her, line by line, to the heights of her capacity. She discovers in the moment a speed of response, an ear for doublethink, a joy in the thrust and parry of moral debate, which transform her in front of our eyes – which of course proves ever more seductive to her predator.

Two years later, I went on a similar voyage with Rosalind, the heroine of *As You Like It*. Tradition has it that this play is a rural romantic romp – two teenage girls escape their authoritarian palace in the city to seek freedom in the uncharted Forest of Arden. They travel in disguise, Rosalind dressing as a man for practical reasons, to protect them on the journey. But she soon discovers that being perceived as a man affords her instant freedoms. When she finds out that the recent object of her passion, Orlando, has also turned up there, she elects to stay in disguise – not merely so that she can continue to frolic around, but because it would now be unbearable for her to return to her perceived female identity, with all its constraints and conventions. With the unwitting Orlando, she embarks on a radical exploration of the nature of male and female expectations of romance and marriage. To this dynamic, electrifying dance, she brings her razor-sharp thought, anarchic humour and a glorious iconoclasm, which resonate vividly with our own times. She is no jokey tomboy, but an irreverent, dazzling nonconformist – and all this can be played with no loss of joy in the love that both she and Orlando melt into at the play's conclusion.

These are just some of Shakespeare's women that I was lucky to be cast as during my time with the RSC.

And what became clear to me was that all these heroines have a limitless capacity to live the lives that Shakespeare gives to his male protagonists – except that they can't, because of the constraints imposed on their gender by contemporary society.

As this delightfully heretical book explores, if left to their own devices and given comparable freedoms, Shakespeare's women would very possibly have made much wiser decisions than his heroes do, with fewer disastrous consequences for the people around them. To play them is to feel from the inside their force, their frustration, their brilliance, their sorrows and anger in servitude and powerlessness, their liberation in love, their humour and wisdom, and their tantalising unpredictability.

It is no coincidence that Shakespeare peopled his plays with women of strength and force of character. For much of his writing life, Elizabeth I was on the throne – a shrewd, highly educated, multi-lingual powerhouse, admired and resourceful. She was also constrained by the manipulations of her courtiers and councillors, and at times both frustrated and freed by the expectations of her gender. It is clear that she was passionate, proud, fearful and ferocious. It could be said that every quality she possessed has found its way into Shakespeare's heroines. Because whatever he thought of her political decision-making, he was writing many of his plays in the bright beam of her influence and patronage.

As this book reveals, the constraints that his women endure, while sometimes punishing, also provide opportunities for them to push back. We see them encountering obstacles and drawing on their richly creative resources to get under, over or around them. Many of them make wonderful role models – when I was playing Rosalind night after night for nearly two years I felt I would never catch up with her. She was forever dancing on the path in front of me – faster, wittier, nimbler of thought. What she taught me still reverberates in my head as I make my way through life. I often realise how much I owe to all the brave, loving, wise, flawed, funny, complicated Shakespeare heroines I have spent time with.

So I am delighted to be asked to write these few words. For all those who feel intimidated at the thought of reading Shakespeare's plays, or who were perhaps put off them at school, this refreshing book does away with all whiffs of academia and brings the women right into our present day. Here they are with their passions and predicaments laid out as we also might experience them – come, be their friends and co-conspirators.

Theatre is about inviting recognition – audiences are beckoned forward, solicited: 'Look! We are not so different ... can you imagine being in this situation? What would you do if you were? Can you identify with this?' This light-hearted and loving roll call – or rôle call – is an exploration of all that it meant to be a woman when Shakespeare was writing, and celebrates the infinite ways in which we are still those people today.

Juliet Stevenson CBE

PREFACE
BY THE ROYAL SHAKESPEARE COMPANY

The Royal Shakespeare Company (RSC) is a leading global theatre company that sparks local, national and international conversations that build connections, create opportunities and bring joy.

We passionately believe that great storytelling can change the world, and that theatre offers its own unique form of storytelling: it's live and shared, and transforms a group of strangers into audiences who, together, experience a story come to life in front of their eyes.

We collaborate with the most exciting artists to tell the stories of our time, and through a range of programmes we nurture the talent of the future. Our transformative Creative Learning and Engagement programmes reach over half a million young people each year.

OUR HISTORY

Our roots lie in the bold vision of a local brewer, Edward Fordham Flower, who in 1879 donated land and launched a campaign to build the Shakespeare Memorial Theatre in Shakespeare's hometown of Stratford-upon-Avon, with his son Charles.

After the original theatre was destroyed by fire, the New Shakespeare Memorial Theatre opened its doors on an adjacent site in 1932, designed by Elisabeth Scott.

The RSC as we know it today was formed by Sir Peter Hall in 1961, and the theatre was renamed the Royal Shakespeare Theatre. Hall's ambition was to produce

PREFACE

new plays alongside those of Shakespeare and his contemporaries.

In 1974, a former rehearsal room in Stratford became The Other Place, the RSC's first studio theatre. In 1986, the Swan Theatre was created from the shell of the original 1879 Shakespeare Memorial Theatre.

We continue to perform on three permanent stages in our home in Stratford-upon-Avon, as well as in London, and in communities and schools across the country and around the world.

WILLIAM SHAKESPEARE

William Shakespeare lived for 52 years. In that time, he produced approximately 40 plays as well as sonnets and poems, which together form the greatest body of work in the English language.

Born in 1564 in Stratford-upon-Avon, he married at the age of 18 and had three children, one of whom died in 1596. Between 1583 and 1592 Shakespeare drops out of sight and speculation as to his activities at this time is rife as people seek to explain the background to his genius.

In 1594 Shakespeare appears in the records of the Lord Chamberlain's Men, working in Shoreditch as an actor and author of plays at the Rose and the Curtain theatres. In 1599 the company moved to the newly built Globe. By 1603 they had acquired royal patronage and became the King's Men on the accession of King James I.

Shakespeare is believed to have produced much of his work between the late 1580s and 1613, when he then retired to Stratford, where he lived until his death in 1616. The precise chronology of his plays is unknown, although there is an accepted order and approximate timescale.

Of his life very little is known. His legacy is his enthralling stories, memorable characters and beautiful, evocative language. As Samuel Johnson wrote, 'His Works may be considered a Map of Life.'

STAGING SHAKESPEARE'S FEMALE CHARACTERS

At the time in which William Shakespeare was writing (c.1580–1616), women were not allowed to perform on stage in theatres, and all female parts would have been played by boy players. Often the female characters in Shakespeare's plays are given less to say than their male counterparts, with Portia (*The Merchant of Venice*; see page 170), Rosalind (*As You Like It*; see page 84) and Innogen (*Cymbeline*; see page 196) being notable exceptions. But compared to his contemporaries, such as Christopher Marlowe and Ben Jonson, Shakespeare wrote a greater number of plays with women in larger roles, with more to say.

When staging Shakespeare's works today, theatre companies embrace interpretive freedom that extends far beyond the original conditions of performance. Contemporary productions recognise that gender need not determine casting. This approach opens Shakespeare's characters to richer, more varied interpretations, while reflecting the diversity of performers and audiences today.

In recent years the RSC has staged a gender-swapped *The Taming of the Shrew* (see page 263) reimagined within a matriarchal society, and a 50/50 gender-split production of *Troilus and Cressida*, as well as casting women in roles traditionally played by

PREFACE

men in *Timon of Athens* and *Titus Andronicus*. Non-binary performers have brought fresh perspectives to productions of *Hamlet* and *Twelfth Night*. More widely, all-male companies such as Propeller echo Shakespeare's own Lord Chamberlain's and King's Men, Phyllida Lloyd directed a trilogy of Shakespeare plays with all-female casts at the Donmar Warehouse, and Michelle Terry played Hamlet at Shakespeare's Globe in her inaugural season as artistic director.

These diverse casting approaches reflect how contemporary theatre invites audiences to move beyond gender assumptions that we might believe are embedded in Shakespeare's texts, revealing new dimensions within his complex characters and making his work more resonant for today's world.

A note on the source text

Character names and quotes in this book are taken from the RSC's *Complete Works* edition, which is based on the First Folio, published in 1623. The First Folio was the first collection of 36 of William Shakespeare's plays, and the main source for 18 works, including *Macbeth*, *The Tempest* and *Twelfth Night*, without which these plays may have been lost. The First Folio was compiled seven years after Shakespeare's death by his friends and fellow actors, John Heminges and Henry Condell, who wanted to produce a 'true and perfect' copy of his plays.

Character names in this book, such as Innogen, Helen and Katherina, sometimes referred to as Imogen, Helena and Katherine in other editions, are true to their representation in the First Folio, as are quotes, punctuation and act and scene numbers.

SHAKESPEARE'S PLAYS

1580–1590

The Taming of the Shrew

1590–1600

Henry VI, Part 2

Henry VI, Part 3

The Two Gentlemen of Verona

Titus Andronicus

Henry VI, Part 1

Richard III

The Comedy of Errors

Love's Labour's Lost

A Midsummer Night's Dream

Romeo and Juliet

Richard II

King John

The Merchant of Venice

Henry IV, Part 1

Henry IV, Part 2

Much Ado About Nothing

Henry V

As You Like It

Julius Caesar

1600–1610

Hamlet

The Merry Wives of Windsor

Twelfth Night

Troilus and Cressida

Othello

Measure for Measure

All's Well That Ends Well

Timon of Athens

King Lear

Macbeth

Antony and Cleopatra

Coriolanus

Pericles

Cymbeline

AFTER 1610

The Winter's Tale

The Tempest

Henry VIII

The Two Noble Kinsmen

INTRODUCTION
BACKWARDS AND IN HEELS

Shakespeare's men are military heroes and dastardly villains. Or they are tortured souls having existential crises. The plays are all about their ambitions and desires, while Shakespeare's female characters are plot devices, or objects of jealousy or desire, who pop up for a scene or two, only to wander off and then faint or drown themselves. That's what some people think of the plays of Mr William Shakespeare. But this view – to use the words of the Bard himself – is nothing but villainous folly and even flat knavery.

Shakespeare's women are bold, brainy, mischievous – and sometimes downright wicked. From clever Rosalind to ruthless Lady Macbeth, via some lesser-known but equally captivating ladies, this book explores the power, passion and most perceptive observations of Shakespeare's female characters. These women are not just part of the plot; they're the driving force behind the action, cracking jokes, taking matters into their own hands and delivering some serious sass to the patriarchy.

The worlds that Shakespeare creates in his plays tend to be full of rules, with pretty rigid social structures. After all, this was the society he and his audiences were familiar with. Whether they aren't allowed to marry the person they love or crave more power or status than they have, Shakespeare's main characters often have to go against authority to get what they want. Which is, of course, so much harder if you are a woman in the 1500s and 1600s.

But this does not mean that Shakespeare's women accept the status quo. They regularly come up with clever ways to escape the limitations placed upon them, figuring out workarounds to get what they want. Sometimes this goes well (see Rosalind, page 84: fun woodland roleplay) and sometimes it does not (see Juliet, page 92: tomb, bad timing). But either way, they have their own ambitions and desires, which they have to be extra-savvy and inventive to achieve. It's a bit like the famous quote about Ginger Rogers doing the same dance moves as Fred Astaire, only backwards and in high heels. To do as well as the guys, these girls have to work twice as hard!

A lot of the melodrama, immaturity and poor decision-making in the plays comes from the male characters. More often than not, women are the sensible ones trying to sort out the mess that has been made. The women often come across as cleverer and more astute than their male counterparts – Helen in *All's Well That Ends Well* (see page 50) miraculously cures a king with no medical training whatsoever! Sometimes they are even powerful in their own right, taking on traditionally 'masculine' roles and kicking ass doing them – like Cleopatra in *Antony and Cleopatra* (see page 58), or Margaret of Anjou (see page 206) in the *Henry* plays. We also often see how qualities traditionally deemed 'feminine', like compassion, kindness and forgiveness, inspire some of the men to behave a bit better.

None of this is to say that these plays are a post-feminist joyride. One of the reasons why we are still reading, performing and talking about them is that they

INTRODUCTION

contain ambiguities. Shakespeare never tells us what to think. And the women in his plays can be just as dastardly and wrong-headed as the men. His works are often categorised as comedies (everyone gets married), tragedies (everyone dies) and histories (there's a war). But some of his plays have been reclassified into what's known as the 'problem plays', like *The Taming of the Shrew* or *Measure for Measure*, because they don't fit neatly into the other categories. The women in these plays, in particular, experience some nasty things, which can be hard to read or watch. But though we might feel uncomfortable at times, that does at least prompt us to ask questions and look at these plays afresh. We can apply our own interpretation and never run out of different things to see.

Shakespeare was working in what we might call a male-dominated industry – there were no named female playwrights whose work was commercially performed, and women weren't allowed on the stage until 50 years after Shakespeare died. But still, he showed that he 'got' women, far better than his contemporaries, by writing bigger female roles with more nuance. Given the environment he worked in, it seems unlikely that he had a lot of close female friends, so maybe he was surrounded by strong women back home in Stratford-upon-Avon? Or perhaps he just worked out that women can be every bit as witty, power-hungry, honourable, villainous, complicated and brave as men? From principled Cordelia (see page 68) to stroppy Hermia (see page 42), sparky Beatrice (see page 26) and majestic Titania (see page 128) – they may not be dancing backwards, but these ladies have got some kick-ass moves.

LADY MACBETH

MACBETH

Frustrated girlboss gone rogue

LOOK LIKE TH' INNOCENT FLOWER, BUT BE THE SERPENT UNDER'T

ACT 1, SCENE 5

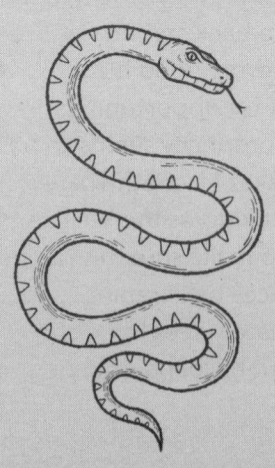

LADY MACBETH

Lady Macbeth is ambitious, smart, passionate and authoritative. She's a strategic thinker and a brilliant speaker – she gets some of the play's best lines. This is a woman who should be a CEO, a start-up founder, a political mover and shaker. But instead, she's trapped in a draughty castle in the middle of nowhere in Scotland with not much to do and with a man she views as a somewhat ineffectual husband. So, when she sees a chance to get some real power and influence for a change, she jumps at it.

As the wife of a minor noble, Lady Macbeth can see all the business of the court being done around her – no doubt far less efficiently than she could do it herself – with apparently no way of getting a seat at the table. While some women would try to reconcile themselves to being the obedient and dutiful wife, that's just not her style at all. Quite rightly, she wants in on the action – although the methods she uses are . . . questionable at best.

For most people, if their other half dropped them a line to say they'd run into some witches on a heath who'd told them all about some upcoming job promotions, they'd be a bit concerned and probably message back something like, 'U OK, hun?' Not so Lady M. Like every good businesswoman, she is always on the lookout for opportunities.

The prophecy seems to be confirmed when the king makes Macbeth Thane of Cawdor. *Could* he be the next king, as the 'weird sisters' said? Lady Macbeth wants to make sure this happens, so when King Duncan announces he's coming for a one-night visit, she immediately sees her opportunity. She hectors her reluctant husband until he agrees to kill him.

WHEN THE LAST PARTY GUESTS HAVE SAID GOODBYE BUT STILL DON'T SEEM TO BE LEAVING:

*Stand not upon
the order of your going,
But go at once.*

WHEN IT'S DEFINITELY TIME
TO CALL IT A NIGHT:

*What's done cannot be undone.
To bed, to bed, to bed.*

THE ULTIMATE LINE FOR WHEN YOU NEED
TO WOMAN UP AND BE BRAVE:

*Screw your courage to
the sticking-place*

LADY MACBETH

While Duncan is asleep, Lady Macbeth gives his guards drugged wine to ensure they won't wake up, so Macbeth can steal in and do the deed. However, he is – understandably – pretty messed up by the whole thing and has kept hold of the daggers he used rather than planting them on the unconscious guards to frame them, as per the plan. 'Give me the daggers,' says Lady M, who goes off to sort it out.

Like in all dark thrillers, one murder leads to another, and then another. First, when the king's death has been discovered, Macbeth kills the guards in a show of righteous retribution. Macbeth does become king, but he is worried about his friend Banquo, who was not only there when the witches delivered their prophecy (and so knows all about it; Macbeth pretends, implausibly, that it's slipped his mind), and whose descendants, it was also foretold, will eventually take the throne. Lady Macbeth thinks they have gone far enough: 'You must leave this,' she tells Macbeth. But, like a gambler who has gone all in, he can only double down. Banquo has to go. The Macduff family fall foul of Macbeth's ambition next, in a bloody massacre of innocent people. It's all got wildly out of hand.

As generations of frustrated, brilliant women would agree, it's more than annoying trying to make it in a man's world, where everyone underestimates you. Not to suggest that she should get away with murder or anything, but Lady Macbeth is trying to operate in a world of warriors and battles, where you take what you want by force. It's all she knows. Even though she has the ambition, drive and ruthlessness that would get her hired at any major corporation, she still sees violence as the only way to get what she wants. To say she has internalised toxic masculinity is probably an understatement. When Macbeth seems to be backtracking on the whole killing-the-king idea, she tells him, 'When you durst do it, then you were a man.' Man up and commit regicide, essentially.

But it's one thing to talk about it, another to do it and live through the consequences. Before Macbeth killed Duncan, Lady M says that she thought she might do the deed herself, but he reminded her of her father, and she couldn't bring herself to do it. As the bloodbath continues, her guilt grows and eventually sends her mad. Stalking her apartments, terrifying the bejesus out of her lady-in-waiting, she is suffering major buyer's remorse. In a scene that has become iconic, she washes her hands over and over, trying to get rid of a bloody 'spot' that only she can see.

In Shakespearean terms, the tragedy of *Macbeth* is the completely avoidable bloodbath caused by ambition and hubris, and the folly of listening to evil supernatural beings. But imagine if, instead of committing murder, going mad and dying by suicide, the motivated and clever Lady Macbeth had got the chance to run Scotland. If she had lived in a time (or a play) where she could have used her talents properly, it all could have been so different, because she is a woman who knows how to get things done.

Ultimately, Lady Macbeth shows that women can be just as – if not more – ambitious than men. And to deny that, to hide or be ashamed of their desire for influence and success, doesn't do anyone any good. Lady Macbeth should have been the ultimate girlboss with her own podcast and TED Talk – not stuck in feudal Scotland serving possets to thanes and soldiers.

RSC STAGE HISTORY

In the 1955 production, famous screen siren Vivien Leigh played an iconic Lady Macbeth opposite her then-husband Laurence Olivier, despite their increasingly troubled marriage. Leigh's costume (still held in the RSC archives) was an amazing dark-green velvet dress and cloak – the bodice had painted-on abdominal muscles! The season featuring Leigh and Olivier was wildly popular with audiences: 500,000 applications were received for 80,000 available tickets before the box office had even opened.

BEATRICE

MUCH ADO ABOUT NOTHING

Sparky queen of put-downs

I HAD RATHER HEAR MY DOG BARK AT A CROW THAN A MAN SWEAR HE LOVES ME.

ACT 1, SCENE 1

BEATRICE

Witty, independent and whip-smart, Beatrice values her friendships and her freedom over any male attention. Benedick, a local lord recently returned from fighting in the war, is irreverent, quick-witted and somewhat arrogant – and swears he will never marry. I think we can all see what's going to happen here.

In theory, the far more conventional relationship between needy, gullible soldier Claudio and Beatrice's best friend/cousin Hero, the daughter of Leonato, governor of Messina, is meant to be the play's focus. But the sparkly verbal sparring between Beatrice and Benedick easily upstages them – this is the couple we care about.

The implication is that they have known each other for a while – and even that Beatrice might have once liked him a teeny-tiny bit (though she could also be joking – Benedick can't tell). She is quick to ask after Benedick when she encounters a messenger just back from the war, although in her standard jokey way, claiming he is a terrible soldier and referencing his professed immunity to falling in love – so it's clearly on her mind. When Benedick then appears, the two fall into what we understand is their familiar mutual piss-taking. He greets her as 'Lady Disdain' and she happily replies that she has plenty of things to be disdainful of when he is around. These guys have serious chemistry.

Beatrice gets away with doing and saying pretty much whatever she wants. It helps that, as the governor's niece, she has a certain social standing and level of privilege, but she flouts social conventions, freely shows how intelligent she is and openly banters with the men around her, even those of higher status than her, like the prince, Don Pedro. And, of course, this is a comedy, not a tragedy. Ophelia (see page 34) would never be able to behave like this at Elsinore Castle. But it's mostly down to her sense of humour and – until later in the play, at least – her cheery good nature. The prince says to her, 'To be merry best becomes you, for out of question, you were born in a merry hour.' She is constantly being asked when she will get married, but – like Bridget Jones centuries later – she bats away the annoying questions with a good joke.

That's not to say that her words don't sting sometimes. At the masked ball thrown by Leonato, she pretends not to recognise Benedick and refers to him as 'the prince's jester, a very dull fool'. 'She speaks poniards [daggers], and every word stabs,' complains Benedick afterwards to Don Pedro – though that doesn't stop him going on and on about her at the slightest provocation.

Having successfully set up Hero and Claudio, who will wed in a week, Don Pedro decides he's going to get Beatrice and Benedick together – and the plan works. By staging a conversation in Benedick's earshot about how Beatrice is secretly in love with him but too proud to admit it, and doing the same to Beatrice, their friends manage to break down the barriers that each has put up and they admit to themselves that they really like each other after all.

However, when sulky misanthrope and self-confessed villain Don John decides to convince Claudio that his fiancée is cheating on him and Claudio leaves Hero at the altar, Beatrice is furious. She doesn't doubt her cousin for a second and yet, as a woman, she knows she is powerless to do anything about the situation.

BEATRICE

WHEN A GUY HAS TREATED YOUR FRIEND BADLY:

Is he not approved in the height a villain, that hath slandered, scorned, dishonoured my kinswoman?

WHEN YOU'RE TRYING TO KEEP IT LIGHT AND AVOID A DEEP AND MEANINGFUL:

I was born to speak all mirth and no matter.

WHEN YOU 'RELUCTANTLY' AGREE TO A COUPLE OF GLASSES OF WINE ON A TUESDAY:

I would not deny you, but by this good day, I yield upon great persuasion.

'O God, that I were a man! I would eat his heart in the market-place,' she cries in frustration.

For some reason, Benedick chooses this moment to tell Beatrice that he is in love with her. Dropping the flirty bickering, she tells him she feels the same – 'I love you with so much of my heart that none is left to protest.' But she wants him to challenge Claudio, his friend, to a duel, because of what he has done to Hero. It's the last thing Benedick wants to do but, reluctantly, he agrees.

This being a comedy, the misunderstanding is soon resolved, Don John is exposed as the culprit, and Hero and Claudio, and Beatrice and Benedick, celebrate a joyful double wedding. Benedick happily admits that he was wrong to say he would never get married and there is every sign that the couple will continue to take the piss out of each other long into a happy old age.

From *His Girl Friday* to *How to Lose a Guy in 10 Days*, *Pride and Prejudice* to *You've Got Mail*, we love a couple who are drawn to each other's wit and whose sharp exteriors conceal a secret romantic heart. And in many ways, Beatrice and Benedick – two avoidant people masking their real feelings for each other – are the blueprint for one of our favourite romcom tropes.

Clever, funny, independent Beatrice knows that you should never feel you have to tone yourself down. She shows us that while you have to be prepared to let your guard down and show vulnerability, when the moment comes, the right person will love you for who you are.

RSC STAGE HISTORY

Meera Syal played Beatrice in the World Shakespeare Festival 2012 production set in modern Delhi, directed by Iqbal Khan. The vibrant set design saw Leonato's house become a rambling traditional *haveli* residence, with balconies, an exterior staircase and even a swing for Beatrice and Benedick to share. Though the wonderfully funny and sharp Syal seems like the perfect actor to play Beatrice, she was in fact initially more interested in playing Katherina from *The Taming of the Shrew*, but as this was already being staged at the festival, Beatrice was decided upon, which Syal later said was actually 'a deeper and richer part.'

OPHELIA

HAMLET

You'd be mad, too

WE KNOW WHAT WE ARE, BUT KNOW NOT WHAT WE MAY BE.

ACT 4, SCENE 4

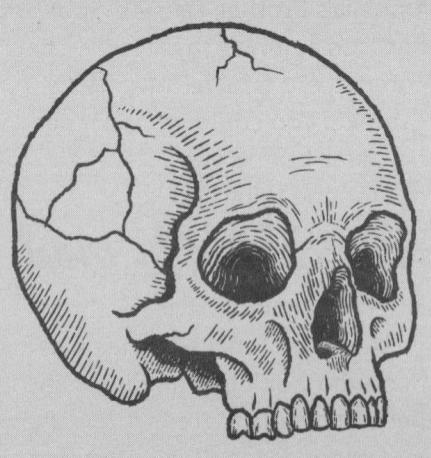

OPHELIA

The conventional reading of *Hamlet* is that it's the tragedy of a tortured soul in the middle of an existential crisis. And, sure, Hamlet is grieving his dead dad whose demise – according to a ghost, that is – occurred in suspicious circumstances. But his behaviour is pretty appalling and, ultimately, it's the women around him who have to put up with it and who suffer the consequences.

It may seem hard to argue that Ophelia is a strong woman, but it's also hardly fair to leave her out. It's more that, in the toxic, misogynistic world of Elsinore Castle, she is constantly denied the chance to know what she wants, let alone go for it. She is doomed from the start.

Ophelia is a good and loyal person who wants to see the best in those around her. She loves her dad, Polonius, even though he's a bit of a pompous old windbag, dishing out nonsensical advice and opinions no one asked for. She likes Hamlet a lot and they seem to have been seeing one another. But according to Ophelia's brother, Laertes, Hamlet is breadcrumbing her. He's a prince, says Laertes, he's not going to commit, etc. (*You're not good enough for him* is the subtext.) You could say that Laertes is looking out for his sister, but his view is that all young men are only out for one thing and it's up to women to guard their reputations at all costs. He says, 'Best safety lies in fear.' So, women should be scared of men, rather than men changing their behaviour? Hmm. Sounds familiar.

Next up, Ophelia is hugely patronised by her dad, who won't listen to what she is saying and calls her a baby and a 'green girl' – she's gullible and inexperienced, basically. But that's nothing compared to the run-in she has with Hamlet. Having been told

WHEN HE ALWAYS REPLIES TO MESSAGES IMMEDIATELY:

You are keen, my lord, you are keen.

WHEN YOU'VE JUST LOOKED IN THE MIRROR THE MORNING AFTER A BIG NIGHT OUT:

*O, woe is me,
T'have seen what I have seen,
see what I see!*

WHEN YOUR FRIENDS HAVE RECOMMENDED A TOTALLY CONFUSING NETFLIX SERIES:

*Will they tell us what
this show meant?*

by the ghost of the dead king that Hamlet's uncle, his dad's brother, was responsible for his recent death, so he could take the throne and marry Hamlet's mum, Hamlet is having quite the meltdown. The way he takes it out on Ophelia is difficult to watch.

Hung up on the idea of his mum having sex with his uncle and feeling rejected by Ophelia, who has given back his love letters because her interfering father told her to, Hamlet goes into full-blown incel mode. He accuses women of pretending to be 'pure' while using their sexuality to manipulate men and of being fundamentally dishonest. Apparently, it's even their fault that there are bad men in the world because they gave birth to them. This is the famous 'get thee to a nunnery' scene where Hamlet blames women for men's bad behaviour. (A nunnery was also Elizabethan slang for a brothel, so either way, he's saying women should be locked away somewhere.) But despite being on the receiving end of this nasty little tantrum, Ophelia reacts with compassion and generosity. She focuses more on how he used to be and is distressed that he seems to have lost his previously 'noble mind'. Understandably, there is only so much one woman can take. Ophelia is surrounded by manipulative misogynists who need to do some serious work on themselves – but presumably therapists are few and far between in Elsinore Castle. While Hamlet pretends to go mad in an attempt to expose his stepfather as a murderer, Ophelia really does go mad following the murder of her father by Hamlet.

One reading of Ophelia's madness in the play is that this is the only dramatic option available if she is to liberate herself from the constant gaslighting and attempted sexual shaming she receives in the claustrophobic world of the Danish court. While she doesn't choose to go mad, when she does, she is able to express how she feels. Now she can say whatever she wants, and she starts singing slightly rude songs about men who sleep with women promising to marry them.

It's not long before Ophelia is found dead. Gertrude breaks the news to Laertes and the king that she has drowned. She describes a romantic scene, Ophelia picking flowers by a picturesque brook, then accidentally falling in and sinking because of the weight of her skirts. It's likely Gertrude frames Ophelia's death like this to try to spare Laertes' feelings and that, in reality, Ophelia chose to die, which is backed up by the priest's refusal to give Ophelia a Christian burial. (Though it has to be said that the idea of death by restrictive, decorative women's clothing feels like one we can all imagine.)

Unlike many of Shakespeare's other female characters, who are able to take some agency in the patriarchal worlds in which they live, even if it still doesn't end well, this kind and hopeful young woman didn't stand a chance. If she was around today, she'd be a singer-songwriter with a huge audience of women nodding along to her heartfelt lyrics. Taylor Swift even wrote a song about her plight: 'The Fate of Ophelia'. But if Ophelia is mad in *Hamlet*, it's the environment around her that makes her so. Even over 400 years ago, in male-dominated Elizabethan England, Shakespeare could see that having to suppress your feelings and desires is an impossible way to live.

RSC STAGE HISTORY

When a 25-year-old Helen Mirren played Ophelia in Trevor Nunn's 1970 production, she depicted the character as playful and sweet at the start of the play – she stuck out her tongue at her brother when their father was giving him advice before he set off on his travels. She and her brother, Laertes (Christopher Gable), played a duet on a lute, as a 'flirtatious double, almost twins' in matching fur-trimmed doublets. The *New York Times* said that Mirren was 'one of the most spirited Ophelias for many a year. In a tastefully low-key production, she stands out as one unwilling to lower her voice.'

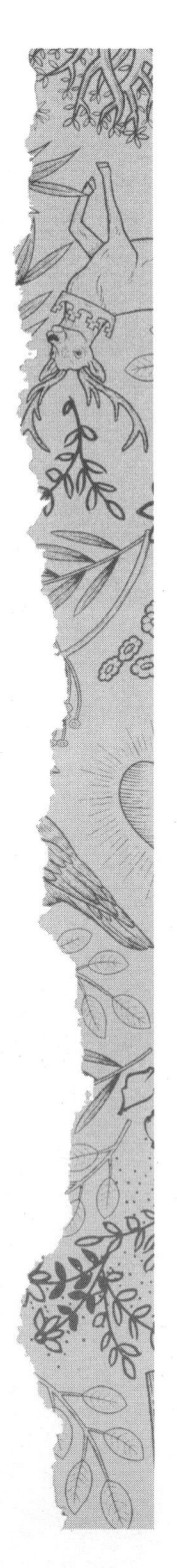

HERMIA AND HELENA

A MIDSUMMER NIGHT'S DREAM

Sisters before misters

LOVE LOOKS NOT WITH THE EYES, BUT WITH THE MIND.

HELENA
ACT 1, SCENE 1

O ME! YOU JUGGLER, YOU CANKER-BLOSSOM, YOU THIEF OF LOVE!

HERMIA
ACT 3, SCENE 2

HERMIA AND HELENA

Who knows what Shakespeare was smoking when he was writing *A Midsummer Night's Dream*, but the result was this mad and enchanting play in which fairies meddle with the emotions of humans to show that love is an irrational, unpredictable, changeable force – however much we feel that it's true, inevitable and everlasting when we fall for someone.

Hermia and Helena have been close friends since childhood, but – as so often happens – then boys get in the way. Demetrius had claimed to be in love with Helena until he met Hermia. But Hermia wants to marry Lysander, not Demetrius. For some reason best known to himself, Hermia's father – another classic meddling dad – is adamant that she has to marry Demetrius and he calls in an even higher male authority, Theseus, Duke of Athens, to back him up. There's an Athenian law that says daughters have to marry who their fathers say, or they will be sent to a convent or, worse, executed. Hermia, in the curt tones used by teenagers throughout history, states that her father doesn't understand her and won't look at the situation from her point of view. The duke backs her dad. But still Hermia isn't going to meekly give in to them – 'My soul consents not to give sovereignty.'

Helena is understandably hurt by the whole situation. Her confidence has been knocked by Demetrius's rejection, and she feels the situation has undermined her friendship with Hermia. When we meet her, she is full of self-pity and wants to know how she can be more like Hermia, if that's what Demetrius is attracted to. Hermia protests that it's not her fault – the ruder she is to Demetrius, the more he follows her around. Which is not the most sympathetic of responses. 'His folly, Helena, is none of mine,' she says, distracted by her own problems.

Hermia and Lysander tell Helena that they are planning on running away. You'd think this would be the best news Helena could have hoped for. With Hermia out of the picture, Demetrius will forget about her and may well remember that it was actually Helena he loved first after all. But – as we see throughout the play – people in love don't always think clearly. And maybe Helena doesn't want to be second best; she wants to be the one Demetrius chooses. So she decides to betray Hermia in an attempt to show Demetrius once and for all that Hermia doesn't love him, and she does. We've all done silly things to make people we fancy like us . . .

The next time we see Helena, it's already clear that the plan was a poor one. She is following Demetrius through the woods and he is – very rudely – trying to get rid of her. But, in full melodramatic mode, Helena is stubbornly refusing to give up. You've got to hand it to her, she is tenacious. 'Your wrongs do set a scandal on my sex,' she cries in frustration. 'We cannot fight for love, as men may do.' But the king of the fairies, Oberon, has seen her distress and feels sorry for her, instructing his fairy servant, Puck, to help out with a little magic.

Little do Demetrius and Helena guess that Puck has put a spell on Lysander (mistaking him for Demetrius), who he has found asleep by himself in the woods. When Lysander wakes up, he declares he's in love with Helena, not Hermia. Now no one is in love with the person who loves them. It's a merry midsummer mess, or an early version of *Made in Chelsea*.

When Puck tries to correct his mistake by also pouring his potion into the eyes of Demetrius, both

WHEN YOU ARE WATCHING
A MANIPULATIVE DATING SHOW:

O hell! To choose love by another's eyes.

WHEN YOU MIGHT BE TOO RELIANT ON
ATTENTION ON SOCIAL MEDIA:

How can it be said I am alone, When all the world is here to look on me?

WHEN YOU THINK YOU MIGHT
HAVE BEEN GHOSTED:

What, out of hearing? Gone? No sound, no word? Alack, where are you?

men think they are now in love with Helena, it's the absolute final straw. They are making fun of her, she thinks. What hurts much more, though, is that she believes her best friend, Hermia, is in on the joke. Sisters don't do this to each other, she says, devastated: 'It is not friendly, 'tis not maidenly. / Our sex, as well as I, may chide you for it.'

It culminates in an almighty, and hilarious, row between Helena and Hermia, who forget the two men as they trade insults, both completely confused and hurt by what they perceive as the other's cruel behaviour.

Puck eventually turns up and sorts it out, leaving Demetrius under the spell so he continues to love Helena (fairies aren't so concerned about free will), and restoring Lysander to his love of Hermia. 'Cupid is a knavish lad. / Thus to make poor females mad,' he says, ignoring the fact that it was he and the two boys who were responsible for the whole situation in the first place.

In a major U-turn, Theseus is now going to allow the couples to get married as they wish, as he can't really be bothered with it all and would rather go hunting. Most importantly, Helena and Hermia become friends again. The key outcome of the evening, it seems, is that Hermia and Helena have seen how much they value their friendship. Romantic love is changeable and unpredictable – who knows if the marriages will work out? – but they will always have each other. Perhaps next midsummer they can stay indoors and avoid those meddling fairies.

RSC STAGE HISTORY

The most iconic production of *A Midsummer Night's Dream* was directed by Peter Brook in 1970, where Frances de la Tour played Helena alongside Mary Rutherford as Hermia. Regarded as one of the most influential Shakespearean productions of the twentieth century, the white-box set, designed by Sally Jacobs, was turned into a fantastical circus space, with the lovers famously suspended from the ceiling on trapezes while asleep in the forest. De la Tour's tall Helena was deemed a 'comic tour de force', playing opposite Ben Kingsley as Demetrius.

HELEN

ALL'S WELL THAT ENDS WELL

Clever, lonely girl has terrible taste in men

OUR REMEDIES OFT IN OURSELVES DO LIE.

ACT 1, SCENE 1

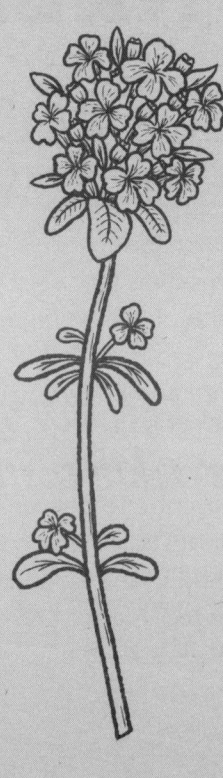

HELEN

All's Well that Ends Well is meant to be a comedy – it has jokes and wordplay, and the plot revolves around marriage, rather than the gruesome death of most of the characters. However, many think it's more of a 'problem play' – one of the darker, morally ambiguous stories that don't fall easily into any other category.

Brave and resourceful, Helen is definitely a strong woman; she's another female protagonist who drives the action and gets what she wants. But it's what – or, more specifically, who – she wants and what she's prepared to do to get him that's the problem.

Helen is the daughter of a famous and well-respected doctor, who has died (we don't know anything about her mother – she's never mentioned). She is young but she must be smart as she has inherited her father's medical knowledge. She lives with the Countess of Rossillion, who acts as her guardian and seems like a good egg.

The problem is, Helen has fallen in love with the countess's son, Bertram, who is not a good egg. He is a spoiled and callous snob, and not into Helen at all. He sees himself as far above her in social standing. On the death of his father, he has become a ward of the French king and is off to join the court in Paris. Helen is devastated and knows her love is one-sided, but she resolves that she has to do something to try to change her situation: 'Our remedies oft in ourselves do lie, / Which we ascribe to heaven.' She's saying that we can change our destinies with our actions, which is punchy in the context of the time, when people believed fervently in providence and God's will – not least because she is a woman.

**WHEN DISCUSSING YOUR
LEAST FAVOURITE POLITICIAN:**

*I know him a notorious liar,
Think him a great way fool,
solely a coward.*

**WHEN DESCRIBING YOUR RELATIONSHIP
WITH YOUR INDIFFERENT KITTY:**

*Yet in this captious
and intenible sieve
I still pour in the
waters of my love*

**WHEN YOU'RE ABSOLUTELY SURE YOURS IS
THE RIGHT WAY TO STACK THE DISHWASHER:**

*If it appear not plain
and prove untrue,
Deadly divorce step
between me and you!*

HELEN

The first part of Helen's plan is to use her understanding of medicine to cure the king of his illness. And, unlike many doctors before her, she manages it! As a reward, she asks for her pick of the courtiers for a husband and the king agrees. No prizes for guessing who she chooses, but Bertram is appalled, and rude: 'A poor physician's daughter my wife? Disdain / Rather corrupt me ever!' The king insists, however, as a point of pride ('My honour's at the stake'), though he also seems to think it's a good match ('She is young, wise, fair').

So does Bertram's mum, the countess, to whom Helen confessed her love before she left for Paris. The countess has great affection for Helen, stressing that she sees her as a daughter. She has no problem with her wanting to marry her beloved son, but Bertram absolutely does. So how are we to take this? When it looks like women in Shakespeare's plays are going to be forced to marry someone, we root for them, hoping they'll be free to choose who they want. Should we want the same for Bertram, or is marrying someone like Helen the best thing that could happen to him?

Although Bertram does agree to marry Helen, he swears to himself that he won't sleep with her. He pretends he'll meet her back at his mother's house but instead runs away to fight in a war, then writes her a nasty, pathetic letter setting out impossible conditions she has to meet if she is to 'call him husband': to get a ring on his finger and get pregnant by him.

You'd think this would be the moment to give up on this terrible idea/man, but Helen just doesn't know how to quit him. (Why, Helen. Why?) Disguised as a pilgrim, she follows him to Florence. When she finds out that Bertram is trying to seduce a young woman called Diana, she gets Diana to give Bertram the ring that Helen got from the king to say thanks for saving his life. So, ring – tick. Then she tricks Bertram into sleeping with her, thinking she is Diana. It's all a bit grim and no one comes out of it looking great, but, lo and behold, Helen is pregnant, so when she gets back to the French court she can both expose Bertram's bad behaviour and prove that she has fulfilled his mad T&Cs.

All's well that ends well? Er, OK.

Why does Helen even want this immature, snobby, selfish man? Is it that she has met so few men that she thinks he is her only hope? Or, while living in his mother's house, did she see some redeeming features in him, giving her faith that he just needs to grow up a bit and they'll be great together? Is she just an obsessive social climber who would mistake *Baby Reindeer* for a dating show?

There are certainly a lot of unanswered questions here. On the one hand, Helen regularly protests that she is hopeless and helpless, all the while scheming to get hold of Bertram once and for all. She might not be one of Shakespeare's most relatable heroines, but she is definitely one of the most fascinating. A bit like Lady Macbeth (see page 18), imagine if she could have channelled her energies into something more worthy of her. Ultimately, when clever, brave Helen ends up with immature, selfish Bertram, you can't help but feel that though this may not be a tragedy, it's definitely a travesty.

RSC STAGE HISTORY

Rosie Sheehy was cast as Helen in Blanche McIntyre's 2022 production, which foregrounded themes of toxic masculinity and unrequited love. Sheehy played Helen as an obsessive schoolgirl with a crush on Bertram (Benjamin Westerby). Robert Innes Hopkins' set projected Instagram messages, digital love hearts and video games, highlighting the characters' self-awareness and the curation of their lives through social media.

CLEOPATRA

ANTONY AND CLEOPATRA

*Powerful queen likes
Roman men and fame*

GIVE ME MY ROBE, PUT ON MY CROWN: I HAVE IMMORTAL LONGINGS IN ME.

ACT 5, SCENE 2

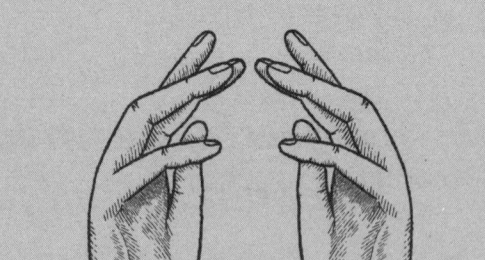

CLEOPATRA

Finally! A female ruler. Not an aspiring power broker or the dutiful wife of a king, but an actual lady in charge. About time, Will. And not only is she a supremely powerful monarch, she's a celebrity, too, famous throughout the Western world (and beyond). As a character she is capricious, complex, ambitious and very sexy. Hold on to your hats, boys.

When it comes to Cleopatra, the buttoned-up Romans just can't even. Theirs is a society of reason and absolute patriarchal control, so, predictably, they are confused by, afraid of and generally quite aroused by this great female ruler in the East. Rome and Egypt are hardly allies, but at the start of the play, there is an uneasy peace between the two. Cleopatra had formerly maintained this through her relationship with Julius Caesar, with whom she had a son (was she allowing him to sleep with her to protect her kingdom or manipulating him with sex? It's yet another ambiguity in this gloriously twisty play). But now Caesar is dead and the Roman Empire is ruled jointly by Mark Antony, Lepidus and Octavius Caesar, JC's nephew and adopted son. Except Mark Antony is now shacked up with Cleopatra in Alexandria, prompting much scandal and gossip back in Rome. Octavius, in particular, is not happy. Nor, presumably, is Antony's wife, Fulvia, but she never appears on stage and dies in Act 2.

> *All the gods go with you.*
> *Upon your sword*
> *Sit laurel victory, and*
> *smooth success*
> *Be strewed before your feet.*
>
> **ACT 1, SCENE 3**

Shakespeare gave Cleopatra 678 lines, second in quantity only to Rosalind in *As You Like It* (see page 84), but even when she's not on stage she seems to dominate the play. Just like any controversial celebrity, people can't stop talking about her and it seems everyone has an opinion. She is described as a 'strumpet', a 'whore', a 'slave' and a 'wrangling queen' by the Romans, who think she is manipulating and emasculating Antony for her own gain, though those who have met her tend to see her differently. Tough old soldier Enobarbus admires her. He poetically tells the story of when Antony and Cleopatra met in a way that implies her grandeur and power, but he stops short of describing the queen herself – 'For her own person, / It beggared all description.' The best he can do is the play's most famous quote about Cleopatra: 'Age cannot wither her, nor custom stale / Her infinite variety.'

It's this 'infinite variety' that makes Cleopatra so interesting. And she does seem strangely ageless; her sex appeal is derived from something much more powerful than youthful good looks. 'Though age from folly could not give me freedom, / It does from childishness,' she says, reflecting on how her love for Antony can make her behave foolishly, though she is no longer childish in her understanding of her emotions.

> *Thou shalt be whipped with wire and stewed in brine, Smarting in ling'ring pickle!*
> ACT 2, SCENE 5

Unlike in many of his other tragedies, Shakespeare doesn't give his characters any soliloquies here. There are no moments when they are alone on stage speaking their thoughts, so we never know what's really going on with Cleopatra. We have to remember that Cleopatra is a queen, a clever politician with a country to run, as well as a woman in love.

> *Eternity was in our lips and eyes, Bliss in our brows' bent: none our parts so poor But was a race of heaven.*
>
> **ACT 1, SCENE 3**

She makes speeches to Antony, assuring him of her devotion, and she reminisces fondly about their fun, sexy times together, like when they got drunk and she made him wear her clothes and she took his famous sword (er, nothing phallic going on here . . .). But there is a slight sense that she wants to see him as an all-conquering hero, a demigod, and the reality never quite lives up to her ideal.

When she learns that Antony has married Octavius's sister, Octavia, on a trip to Rome, Cleopatra is furious – maybe more angry than hurt, in fact? In a scene we probably all recognise even if we don't want to admit it, she grills another messenger about Octavia's beauty and is happy to hear that her rival is *not as hot as you, your highness*, to paraphrase.

Despite his expedient marriage to Octavius's sister, Antony soon falls out with Octavius. An ill-advised sea battle is arranged – Romans versus Egyptians, with Antony commanding the Egyptian ships. But when Cleopatra's ships run away, Antony decides to follow her. It's a decisive moment, which seems to confirm what the Romans believe: that Antony is in thrall to

WHEN YOU DECIDE TO PLAY DUMB TO GET OUT OF A WORK ASSIGNMENT:

I'll seem the fool I am not.

WHEN YOU WANT INTEL ON A CRUSH:

*See where he is,
who's with him, what he does.
I did not send you.*

WHEN YOUR BEST WORK BUDDY ANNOUNCES THEY ARE QUITTING:

*Hast thou no care of me?
Shall I abide
In this dull world, which
in thy absence is
No better than a sty?*

this 'witch' from the East and has lost all his manly ability as a soldier.

Why does Cleopatra order the retreat? We don't know. She could have got cold feet or decided that Antony's was the losing side and she would do better to make an alliance with Octavius. Maybe she's still annoyed about the marriage thing. Antony is humiliated and decides to fight Octavius's troops again, on land this time. He wins, but there is no turning the tide. His men have lost all faith in him and they begin deserting. Antony then loses a third battle and Cleopatra retreats to her 'monument' – a tomb, basically.

While giving each other some space at this point does seem a good idea, where Antony is concerned Cleopatra seems incapable of restraint. She tries to get his attention by making him think she is dead. It all goes horribly, predictably wrong and – sad and embarrassed by his failures – Antony 'falls on his sword'. Even this doesn't work out as he had hoped, and he fails to die straight away. A messenger discovers him, and he is taken to Cleopatra to die in her arms.

Octavius is desperate to capture Cleopatra and take her back to Rome, to show off how clever he is to have defeated the powerful, attractive witch, but Cleopatra is not going to let that happen. She also doesn't want Antony's widow, Octavia, to have the pleasure of seeing her defeated. Always loving a bit of regal drama, she gets all dressed up in her finest clothes and lets a poisonous snake bite her, bringing about her death.

Octavius declares that Cleopatra and Antony will be buried in the same grave – though 'No grave upon

> *My salad days,*
> *When I was*
> *green in*
> *judgement, cold*
> *in blood.*
>
> **ACT 1, SCENE 5**

the earth shall clip in it / A pair so famous.' He may have won the war, but these lovers, he has to admit, have achieved something greater: immortality in their fame and celebrity.

And that's what these two really wanted, as much or maybe more than each other. Especially Cleopatra. And, of course, she gets her way. Shakespeare has at last given us a great female leader, fascinating in her complexity and sexy as hell to boot.

RSC STAGE HISTORY

Janet Suzman played a highly intelligent, athletic Cleopatra in Trevor Nunn's 1972 production, which played in London and was later recorded for television. Richard Johnson played her Antony, while Patrick Stewart played Enobarbus, which he played again in a separate production at the RSC in 1978. Suzman said of her fascination with the role of Cleopatra, versus other Shakespearean women: 'There's not one, I think, that stands where she does in the canon.'

CORDELIA

KING LEAR

*Loyal daughter
refuses to compromise*

I AM SURE MY LOVE'S MORE PONDEROUS THAN MY TONGUE.

ACT 1, SCENE 1

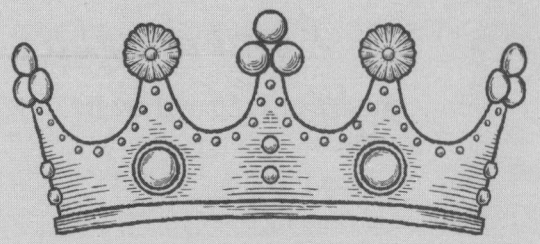

CORDELIA

Girls, *tell me how much you love me*, says King Lear to his three daughters in Act 1, Scene 1, *and I will give you each a third of my kingdom*. Lear is getting on a bit and looking to downsize. He's decided to give them their inheritance early so that 'future strife / May be prevented now'. If only.

Goneril and Regan, his two eldest daughters, have no problem with this. Goneril claims that she loves her father more than words can say, that the depth of her affection makes 'speech unable' – though this doesn't stop her delivering a speech full of words about how much she loves him. It's obvious to the audience – if not to Lear – that what Goneril is saying is over the top and insincere.

Yup, what she said, but even more so, says Regan. And both are each given a third of Britain to rule over, with their husbands.

Cordelia, the youngest sister, refuses to play the game. She is honest, highly moral and loyal – and she can't bring herself to say a load of empty words to prove her daughterly love for her dad. To her, that's not how love works. Lear completely misunderstands her. He is used to obedience and can't tell the difference between empty sycophancy and genuine care. And so begins a whole tragedy based on a father and daughter with different love languages.

Cordelia is disinherited and banished with immediate effect, though there is a silver lining. There are two men who want to marry her: the Duke of Burgundy and the King of France. When they find out that she isn't going to inherit anything from her father, Burgundy loses interest, while the King of France understands that the whole debacle speaks volumes

WHEN YOU SET UP TWO OF YOUR FRIENDS WITH DISASTROUS RESULTS:

*We are not the first
Who with best meaning have
incurred the worst.*

WHEN THE WEATHER TURNS BAD AND YOU NEED TO UP YOUR SKINCARE GAME:

*Was this a face
To be opposed against
the jarring winds?*

WHEN IT'S MORE IMPORTANT TO OFFER SUPPORT THAN ADVICE:

Love and be silent.

about Cordelia's honesty and integrity. He declares that he doesn't care that she doesn't have a dowry and will marry her anyway. So at least Cordelia ends up with someone who values her.

Lear strops off and Cordelia shows that she understands what her sisters are really like. Though she asks them to please look after their dad, in keeping with how much they claimed to love him in their overblown speeches, it's clear she doesn't have much faith in them. And she's right, of course. Lear has 'the unruly waywardness that infirm and choleric years bring with them', agree the two sisters when Cordelia has gone. Though he was always a bit of a stubborn pain in the ass even when he was younger, they say.

All of this happens in the first scene. It's a gripping, cold opener that sets up the conspiracies, betrayal and the decline of the title character, Lear, that are to come. We don't see Cordelia again until Act 4, but her reluctance – or inability – to take part in exaggerated, inauthentic declarations of filial love has consequences that reverberate around the action in her absence.

While Cordelia's sisters are absolutely horrible, they make for compelling viewing. Goneril and Regan are clearly set up as the antithesis to principled Cordelia – though it is kind of thrilling how they go against everything a 'virtuous' woman was supposed to be and do. They are power-obsessed, violent, cruel and horny, too, refusing to submit to the authority of their father or their husbands – Goneril even plots the death of hers. Regan isolates Lear by removing his retinue of knights and putting his loyal servant in the stocks, then they both turn him out in the middle of a storm. They encourage Regan's husband to blind the Earl of

Gloucester in a particularly gory scene where Regan cheers him on, and they both have the hots for Gloucester's illegitimate son, the calculating wrong 'un Edmund.

While Cordelia could have been forgiven for washing her hands of the lot of them and enjoying her new life in France, her loyalty to her father is too strong. Having heard about what her sisters have been up to, she's back – and she's brought an army. But Goneril and Regan have their own soldiers, and it looks like there's going to be a battle.

Unlike her sisters, Cordelia only cares about the wellbeing of her dad. But even though he's realised what a horrible mistake he made in believing his elder daughters' words of love for him, he now won't see his younger daughter as he's too ashamed of his behaviour. When they finally reunite, Lear is confused and ill, and Cordelia is kind to him, putting into action what she tried to tell him in Act 1 – that love isn't about grand statements, but what you do for those you care about.

Despite having grown up in a family that may have inspired the Roys in *Succession*, Cordelia has an unshakeable belief in what is right and the strength of character to stick to this belief, no matter what. While Goneril poisons Regan and then kills herself, Lear dies broken-hearted after Cordelia is captured and killed by Edmund. Audiences are left seeing Cordelia as a paragon of virtue and her death as a tragedy.

Could all this have been avoided if Cordelia had just told her dad what he wanted to hear at the outset and then invited him to live with her in her third of the kingdom? Maybe her life would have been saved had she placated his ego? Or perhaps her evil sisters would have just found another way to get the power they wanted? Who knows. You can't help but think, though, that the court of Queen Cordelia would have been a fair, honest and pleasant place to live.

RSC STAGE HISTORY

Diana Rigg played Cordelia aged 24 in director and designer Peter Brook's landmark 1962 production with Paul Scofield as Lear. Scofield's portrayal of an unsentimental Lear was deemed 'the finest performance ever on the RSC stage' in a 2004 poll with RSC actors. When the production was on tour in 1963, Diana Rigg was embraced backstage in Paris by an excitable Marlene Dietrich, where the show had played to a sold-out Théâtre des Nations.

ADRIANA

THE COMEDY OF ERRORS

Frustrated wife has had it up to here

WHY SHOULD THEIR LIBERTY THAN OURS BE MORE?

ACT 2, SCENE 1

ADRIANA

It's just a normal day in the Greek city of Ephesus for Adriana, who is waiting for her husband, Antipholus, to come home for lunch. He is late, as usual, and Adriana is annoyed. Her sister, Luciana, is trying to placate her. *Well, that's men for you!* she says. They just do what they want and, as women, we just have to put up with it. But Adriana is not having it. 'There's none but asses will be bridled so,' she bristles.

There's something really quite modern about Adriana. In a slightly silly play, she is a figure of exasperated commonsense who finds herself trying to sort out mad messes not of her own making. Audiences at the time might have thought her view that she is entitled to a certain amount of love and respect from her husband unreasonable, but we aren't encouraged to laugh at her for being 'shrewish' or nagging. In fact, it's her loyalty to Antipholus and willingness to take matters into her own hands that helps set right the 'errors' of the play.

It's hard not to feel sorry for Adriana. Things have not been good with her husband for a while. She's worried he's being unfaithful, that he's gone off her and she's got no chance of getting him back while he's out gallivanting and she's stuck at home, trapped being a wife. The final straw comes when her servant Dromio turns up to say that not only is his master not coming home, but he's given him a beating and denied even having a home and a wife. Hurt but refusing to just accept the situation, Adriana decides she's going to locate the errant Antipholus and give him what for. When she finds him in the market, she calls him out on his behaviour. *You used to love me*, she says, *and you would go nuts if I was cheating on you. I am no better than the best part of you, so if you are having an affair then that corrupts and ruins me, too*: 'I do digest the poison of thy flesh, / Being strumpeted by thy contagion.' It's a heartfelt, dignified and moving speech.

However, it doesn't have the desired effect. The problem Adriana has is that, unbeknown to her, the man she is addressing is not her husband but his identical twin – with the same name. Yup. And the servant who is standing in front of her now with his master is not her Dromio, who had attempted to get her 'husband' to come home, but her servant's identical twin, who is her husband's servant's long-lost brother. They, too, have the same name. Keeping up? Good.

This new Antipholus does know he has a twin brother – he's been travelling far and wide trying to find him – so you would think the penny might drop, but no. And so follows a series of misunderstandings and miscommunications where the two Antipholuses inadvertently swap places and no one is talking to the person they think they are.

Luciana tells Adriana that her 'husband' was hitting on her (it was of course his brother), to which Adriana responds with a wonderful tirade of insults directed at her other other half ('He is deformed, crooked, old, and sere / Ill-faced, worse bodied, shapeless everywhere '). Just then, one of the Dromios turns up to ask her for some money to bail her husband out of prison, where he has been sent for non-payment of a debt to the goldsmith, who can't understand why his client is claiming not to have received the jewellery he definitely gave him. Despite her hurt and outrage at what she's just heard, Adriana lets whichever Dromio this is have the money. She is loyal to her husband to a

ADRIANA

WHEN SOMEONE IS BEHAVING OUT OF CHARACTER:

*O, how comes it,
That thou art then
estrangèd from thyself?*

WHEN DEALING WITH A NARKY TRAFFIC WARDEN:

*What wilt thou do,
thou peevish officer?*

A GREAT RUN OF INSULTS TO LET RIP WITH:

*He is deformèd,
crooked, old and sere,
Ill-faced, worse bodied,
shapeless everywhere,
Vicious, ungentle,
foolish, blunt, unkind,
Stigmatical in making,
worse in mind.*

fault, though she is beginning to think that Antipholus has lost the plot. While the audience wonders if *anyone* can follow this plot.

Rather than washing her hands of him, Adriana even finds a doctor to try to help her husband – although maybe part of her hopes that Antipholus has gone mad, as the alternative is that he's just a reckless man who not only doesn't love her anymore, but has no regard for her feelings.

The big reveal happens at a monastery, where one Antipholus has gone to hide after escaping from prison. Still hoping to sort out this mess, Adriana tries to persuade the abbess to let her in. She finds herself on the receiving end of a telling off from the abbess for 'making' her husband unfaithful *and* for having a go at him for cheating on her, as that's probably what made him mad. Not a great look for the sisterhood.

Anyway, the two sets of twins are finally in the same place at the same time, and, with the help of an old man, Egeon, who is the dad of the two Antipholuses, it finally all makes sense. Well, to a point. Oh, and the Antipholus twins' mother turns out to be the very same abbess who moments earlier had been berating Adriana. Presumably Adriana is thrilled at the acquisition of this new mother-in-law.

No matter what was thrown at her, Adriana rolled up her sleeves and tried to sort it out. Even while suffering the very relatable sadness and low self-esteem of a woman who knows her relationship is falling apart but doesn't know what to do about it, she didn't give up, remaining proactive, funny and pleasingly bossy. Let's hope Antipholus realises her value and stops going off for dinner with courtesans.

RSC STAGE HISTORY

In Phillip Breen's outdoor production of *The Comedy of Errors* in 2021, actor Hedydd Dylan was cast as Adriana, but then subsequently became pregnant. The pregnancy was woven in to become part of the character, adding an extra dimension to the role by raising the stakes of her fraught relationship with Antipholus, then heightening the family reunions at the end of the play. Dylan later went on maternity leave and Naomi Sheldon, a recent mother herself, took over the role for the show's transfer to London.

ROSALIND

AS YOU LIKE IT

*Rules are there
to be broken*

I PRAY YOU DO NOT FALL IN LOVE WITH ME, FOR I AM FALSER THAN VOWS MADE IN WINE.

ACT 3, SCENE 5

ROSALIND

There's a strong case to be made that Rosalind is Shakespeare's most modern heroine. Like Viola (see page 144) and Portia (see page 170), she disguises herself as a man and thus avoids the restrictions society places on her as a woman. But unlike Viola, who has to react to the wishes of others, or Portia, who assumes male authority for just one key scene, Rosalind drives events throughout *As You Like It* by her decisive action. She also has more lines than any other Shakespearean woman, which allows us to get to know this witty and self-aware, brave and vulnerable, fun and caring woman better.

The play starts by revealing that some emotionally dysregulated men have caused a problem that the women must deal with. How unusual. Rosalind's uncle, Duke Frederick, has banished her dad, Duke Senior, to the Forest of Arden. (Where, according to Charles the wrestler, there are 'many merry men with him; and there they live like the old Robin Hood of England'. Which sounds fun.) Sensibly, Rosalind and her cousin Celia won't let their fathers' tiff impact their friendship.

Meanwhile, Orlando is at odds with his brother, Oliver, who irrationally loathes him and won't give him his share of their father's inheritance. Rosalind and Celia, ever compassionate and wise, try to talk Orlando, who they have not met before, out of a wrestling match with burly Charles, who Oliver hopes will finish him off. But with equal parts self-pity and bravery, Orlando goes ahead. Miraculously, he wins, Rosalind congratulates him and – bang – they are in love.

Next, the cantankerous Duke Frederick suddenly banishes Rosalind, too. She and Celia decide to go to the forest to look for Rosalind's father (do they know

WHEN YOU'RE TRYING TO BE HAPPY
ABOUT A FRIEND'S NEW KITCHEN, EVEN
THOUGH YOURS IS FALLING APART:

*Well, I will forget the condition
of my estate, to rejoice in yours.*

TO YOUR FRIEND, WHO HAS BEEN TRYING
TO RESIST GIVING THEIR OPINION:

Now unmuzzle your wisdom.

WHEN YOU'VE HAD ONE TOO MANY RUN-INS
WITH A PRICKLY COLLEAGUE:

*O, how full of briars is this
working-day world!*

about the 'many merry men'?). For safety, Rosalind, who is taller, will dress as a man called Ganymede, while Celia will pretend to be his sister. So off they go, with the fool Touchstone, and buy a cottage and land in no time. These women know how to make things happen.

While walking in the woods, Rosalind (as Ganymede) finds some bad love poetry about her pinned to the trees. Celia has seen the man who wrote it. The culprit – sorry, author – is Orlando, who is also living in the forest, having worked out that his brother would prefer him dead. Rosalind asks all the usual questions when your friend runs into someone you fancy – *where did you see him? How did he look? Did he ask after me? Does he know I am in the forest dressed like a bloke?* (OK, maybe not the last one.) Celia is amused by her cousin's agitation.

Luckily, Rosalind has got it together by the time she sees Orlando. Thanks to her disguise, she can boldly ask him if he loves Rosalind, while posing as a cheeky woods chappie who is improbably well-spoken. *Er, I had a posh uncle who taught me to speak*, says Rosalind/Ganymede. She tells him she can cure his lovesickness through roleplay if he will stop by the cottage every day. As with Orsino and Viola in *Twelfth Night*, sidestepping gendered social conventions means the couple can spend time together in a more honest, open way. As we often see in Shakespeare's plays, being false can enable you to be truer.

Orlando might have decided that he is hopelessly, carving-her-name-into-tree-trunks in love with Rosalind after only one meeting, but she's more practical and realistic and needs to know whether he is more than a terrible poet and reasonable wrestler.

Orlando declares he would die if Rosalind said she didn't love him. Rosalind has no time for this kind of performative melodrama. *No one really dies from a broken heart,* Ganymede tells him firmly. She has a lot of fun winding him up about married life. 'And wilt thou have me?' Orlando asks pretend/real Rosalind. 'Ay, and twenty such,' she responds. *Whaaaat?* he says, confused. *Well, you're a good man, right? And you can't have too much of a good thing!* she comes back wittily.

The lack of male authority figures in the less-rule-bound forest means that Rosalind and Celia can do what they like, but the fun can't last forever. First, Phoebe, a shepherdess who their friend Silvius really wants to marry, decides she is in love with Ganymede (awkward). Then Orlando's formerly nasty brother Oliver turns up to say a) he's no longer a bastard, and b) Orlando has been bitten by a lion while saving Oliver's life. Plus, there's the matter of Rosalind's dad camped out nearby. Rosalind can see things are getting out of hand and decides it's time she fixes it all.

So, Rosalind (as Ganymede) gathers everyone at her father's outlaw court and asks him, if Rosalind shows up, can she marry Orlando? *Sure!* he says. When she returns as Rosalind, with Celia and Hymen, the goddess of marriage (just go with it), she marries Orlando, Celia marries the reformed Oliver, Touchstone marries a goatherd called Audrey, and Phoebe is tricked into marrying Silvius. We'll have to hope for the best there.

The last words are Rosalind's, who addresses the audience in a witty, teasing note, acknowledging it is 'not the fashion to see the lady the epilogue'. Rosalind has no time for convention, skipping around the patriarchy to do exactly as she wishes.

RSC STAGE HISTORY

A 24-year-old Vanessa Redgrave dominated Michael Elliott's 1961 production of *As You Like It* with her luminous performance, which gained universal praise. Theatre critic Michael Billington said of her performance that 'Critics, mostly male, fell in love on the spot' at the moment when Rosalind, dressed as Ganymede, fell down in ecstasy in her passion for Orlando. It was the RSC's first production of the play as the company gained its royal status in 1961. The production was adapted for the BBC and televised in 1963.

JULIET

ROMEO AND JULIET

Aspiring romcom heroine dealt a terrible hand

MY ONLY LOVE SPRUNG FROM MY ONLY HATE!

ACT 1, SCENE 4

JULIET

Passionate, flirty, clever and headstrong, had Juliet Capulet found herself in one of Shakespeare's comedies where she could have received a better ending, she might have been the original romcom heroine. Still, even as one half of the most famous 'star-crossed lovers' of all time, she has a lot to show us about being open to love, following your heart and judging someone by who they are and not where they come from.

Romeo and Juliet's meet-cute happens at a party thrown by Juliet's dad. But, as in many romantic tales, when our protagonists first lay eyes on one another, they are both sort of involved with other people. Romeo won't stop telling his friends about his infatuation with someone called Rosaline, though she is clearly not into him. While Juliet has received a proposal from the good-looking and rich Count Paris, and is coming under increasing pressure from her parents to marry him. (Lord Capulet seems to be quite taken with Paris himself, describing him as 'Proportioned as one's thoughts would wish a man'. Er, do you mean he is . . . tall, sir?)

If we're being totally honest, Romeo comes with enough red flags to make a string of bunting. Just for a start, there's the way he forgets about Rosaline immediately after seeing Juliet, having literally just declared that no woman on Earth could be her equal. (He also refuses to dance at the party and insists on telling his friends

Parting is such sweet sorrow, That I shall say goodnight till it be morrow.

ACT 2, SCENE 1

> *My bounty is as boundless as the sea, My love as deep: the more I give to thee, The more I have, for both are infinite.*
>
> **ACT 2, SCENE 1**

about his dream on the way there – dude, no one wants to hear about your dream.) But the biggie is, of course, the ongoing violent feud between his family, the Montagues, and Juliet's clan, the Capulets, which culminates in Romeo killing Tybalt, Juliet's beloved cousin, straight after R&J's whirlwind secret marriage. Awkward!

And yet the main reason why we root for these two people, why we believe that they have fallen instantly in love with one another and why Shakespeare's *Romeo and Juliet* has inspired so many love-across-the-divide stories, is Juliet herself.

Juliet is only 13, which feels very problematic to us now, but audiences at the time would have thought this very young, too – the average age of marriage in Shakespeare's day was around 20. It's possible that Shakespeare made Romeo and Juliet so young for dramatic effect; to highlight youthful passion, innocence and impulsivity and to make the play's outcome even more tragic. And yet, despite Juliet's age, she knows her own mind. She has enough self-belief to defy her parents, even when her dad threatens to throw her out of the house for refusing to marry the perfectly proportioned Paris. She's quite rightly annoyed that Paris claims to be so keen to marry her and yet has proposed through her parents, without even bothering to try to charm her in person – 'I wonder at this haste, that I must wed / Ere he that should be husband comes to woo.' She sees him for what he is: an entitled man who can't read the room.

Juliet is sassy and funny, too – exactly as we want our female romantic leads to be. When she runs into Paris on her way to see Friar Laurence, who is willing to help the two young lovers be together, she is sarcastic and cutting, though it mostly goes over his head.

Most importantly, Juliet is straightforward and direct in her dealings with Romeo. They flirt hard but she checks him when his declarations of love start to sound like meaningless, overblown romantic statements. She makes sure she focuses on the real feelings between them. Juliet is the first to suggest that they get married – but she sends Romeo away to think about it and tells him to let her know in the morning.

> *So tedious is this day*
> *As is the night before*
> *some festival*
> *To an impatient child*
> *that hath new robes*
> *And may not wear*
> *them.*
>
> **ACT 3, SCENE 2**

When Juliet learns of the circumstances of Tybalt's death, she doesn't stick her head in the sand and make excuses for the now-exiled Romeo. She is initially furious with him, but Juliet is a realist – she knows that Tybalt had it in for Romeo and would have killed him, too. It's a tough call, but she chooses Romeo over her dysfunctional family – though she has just married him, so she doesn't have a lot of choice. However, seeing her faith in him, the audience feels it, too – and it does help that we know Tybalt was

SHAKESPEARE'S STRONG WOMEN

WHEN THE REALLY HOT GUY TURNS OUT TO BE A LYING SCUMBAG:

*Was ever book containing
such vile matter
So fairly bound?
O, that deceit should dwell
In such a gorgeous palace!*

WHEN YOU REALISE IT'S ALL GOING A BIT TOO FAST AND YOU NEED A TIME-OUT:

*Although I joy in thee,
I have no joy of
this contract tonight:
It is too rash, too unadvised,
too sudden.*

WHEN YOUR ALARM GOES OFF AT 7 A.M. ON A MONDAY:

*Dreadful trumpet, sound the
general doom.*

an aggressive thug who was in need of some anger-management therapy.

And although it's Friar Laurence who comes up with the plan of Juliet faking her death by taking a strong sleeping draught, she is the one who has to see it through. She's scared that it won't work at all and she'll have to marry Paris, or she will wake up alone and terrified in a creepy crypt – possibly next to the recently dead Tybalt. Grim. For a moment, she even worries that Friar Laurence might be trying to poison her to cover up the fact that he has already married her to Romeo against her father's wishes. But Juliet is tough and she downs the contents of the vial, drinking a toast to her love.

> *What's in a name? That which we call a rose By any other word would smell as sweet.*
>
> **ACT 2, SCENE 1**

If we could stop the play before the final scene, or perhaps if there had been a reliable postal service between Verona and Mantua, where Romeo is exiled, then we could imagine another resolution for the famous lovers. In our alternative romcom ending, maybe Juliet would wake up in time and the couple could skip out on their bickering families and spend the summer backpacking around Italy, picking up shifts in tavernas and alehouses. But, alas, Shakespeare decided to write a tragedy, and so we have to sob our way through the famous scene of Romeo dying from taking poison just as Juliet comes round.

We are warned right at the beginning of the play about the 'fearful passage of their death-marked love', but for someone doomed by fate and the history of her family's ongoing war with a rival clan, Juliet manages to take a hell of a lot of agency for herself. Her actions and decisions drive the story more than anyone else's, including Romeo's. In the context of a stage tragedy, her decision to stab herself is bold as well as shocking. She believes wholeheartedly in love and has the courage of her convictions right to the end.

RSC STAGE HISTORY

In 2011, Royal Mail celebrated the RSC's fiftieth anniversary by issuing a new set of ten stamps commemorating key productions. The £1.10 stamp featured Francesca Annis as Juliet and Ian McKellen as Romeo in Trevor Nunn's 1976 production. For the production, the RSC's stage and auditorium was transformed into an Elizabethan-style playhouse. Theatre-goers sat in extended wooden galleries surrounding the acting space, giving a sense of what it would have been like to watch a performance in Shakespeare's day. Annis later said that she 'adored' Juliet's 'optimistic determination', and that working with McKellen as Romeo 'had a profound effect' on her.

OLIVIA

TWELFTH NIGHT

Bereaved aristocrat seeks hot . . . guy?

I AM AS MAD AS HE, IF SAD AND MERRY MADNESS EQUAL BE

ACT 3, SCENE 4

OLIVIA

In the last 12 months, Olivia has lost both her brother and her dad. Their deaths have left her a wealthy – if perhaps lonely – heiress who will at least be able to choose who she marries. And her choice is . . . no one. Her lady's maid has revealed that Olivia plans to grieve for seven years, wearing a veil and keeping mostly to herself.

That's a long time to stay single. Is it a reflection of how sad she is, or is she just fed up of being badgered by Orsino and so has developed a low opinion of men generally? Certainly, the men around her are enough to put anyone off dating. Her uncle, the unappealingly named Sir Toby Belch, is a drunken chancer. His mate, Sir Andrew Aguecheek, is ineffectual and vainly thinks he has a chance with Olivia. The two crash around boozily like a Shakespearean Withnail and Marwood.

So when a somewhat arrogant 'fair young man' turns up at Olivia's door demanding to see her, it's not entirely surprising that she is intrigued. She's not made of stone, after all. Her encounter with Viola (see page 144), cosplaying as male page Cesario, makes for a great scene, with an underlying current of sexual tension. There's something appealingly enigmatic about this young man, which Olivia can't quite put her finger on . . .

Viola has characteristically decided that she has to brazen it out if she is going to get anywhere as a fake page. 'The honourable lady of the house, which is she?' she demands, as Cesario, which is of course no way to speak to an honourable lady of any house. When she admits that she doesn't want to start on her carefully memorised speech on behalf of her employer if she's not talking to the right person, Olivia is amused by the candour. She tells Viola to skip the bit of the message that is praise for her and get to the point.

WHEN YOU ARE CALLING IN SICK, HAVING BEEN OUT AT A WORK EVENT THE NIGHT BEFORE:

Even so quickly may one catch the plague?

WHEN YOUR FRIEND IS BEING OVERSENSITIVE:

To be generous, guiltless and of free disposition, is to take those things for bird-bolts that you deem cannon-bullets.

WHEN YOU ARE TOO PREMENSTRUAL TO HANDLE A FRIEND'S EXCITABLE CHAT:

'Tis not that time of moon with me to make one in so skipping a dialogue.

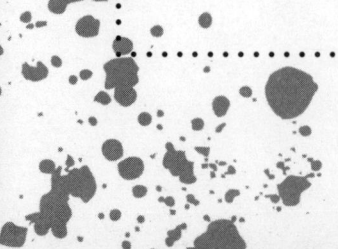

OLIVIA

Olivia sends her attendants away so they are alone, then repeatedly tries to get a sense of who this enigmatic Cesario is and where he comes from (including his 'parentage' – is she already thinking of him as a potential partner?). Does she suspect Cesario is really a woman? Probably not consciously, although perhaps she's picking up on a certain feminine energy – the conversation feels like a frank talk between two women about a man, while at the same time Olivia is coming to the realisation that she fancies this boy... girl... who cares?

Of course, for Shakespeare's audiences, there was an extra layer to all this. Viola, and all other young female characters, would have been played by a young man, maybe a teenage boy, as women were not allowed on the stage. So the actor would have been a boy playing a girl playing a boy. For theatregoers at the time this was normal. They would have suspended their disbelief, just as they accepted that Macbeth could see a floating dagger or Puck could fly. But to the no-fun Puritans of the era, this gender-swapping was dangerous, stirring up all the 'wrong' sorts of feelings in male audience members. So there was an air of transgression to gender-swapping, which Viola and Olivia's scene may be tapping into.

The time between Christmas and New Year was when Elizabethans loosened their ruffs and let their hair down. The last day of this period was known as Twelfth Night, when the usual rules were ignored or turned upside down – including men dressing as women. It was a safe kind of chaos, because everyone knew that the conventions of normal life would return the next day.

The topsy-turvy world of *Twelfth Night* the play (as well as wealth and status) allows Olivia to make all her own decisions. She knows what she wants and is happy to ask for it. She makes her feelings very clear

> *Ungracious wretch,*
> *Fit for the mountains*
> *and the barbarous caves,*
> *Where manners ne'er*
> *were preach'd!*
>
> **ACT 4, SCENE 1**

to Viola (as Cesario) the next time Orsino sends her to press his suit. And later, thinking he is Cesario, she uses her natural authority to rescue Viola's twin, Sebastian, from attack by the idiotic Sir Andrew and Sir Toby, then immediately decides to take him home with her. 'Would thou'dst be ruled by me!' she says, before informing him they are getting married. Of course, in the real world, as a woman, she would be ruled by her husband.

Olivia's eventual marriage to Sebastian neatly resolves the question of her attraction to Viola – although not completely, as when they met she seemed taken not just with Viola's physical appearance, but with her spirited way of talking. Sebastian may look the same as Viola in drag, but he is not the same person. Chemistry is more than just looks.

Ultimately, though, Olivia chooses the person she wants and seems unconcerned that she fell for the sister and has ended up with the brother. The person who deserves a resolution but doesn't get one, however, is Antonio, who rescues Sebastian from the sea and seems to fall in love with him, following him to Illyria. We know that Olivia is pretty open-minded, though, so perhaps he can move into her big house too . . .

RSC STAGE HISTORY

Freema Agyeman played a grieving yet lusty Olivia in Prasanna Puwanarajah's 2024–25 production at the Royal Shakespeare Theatre and the Barbican, London. The production was set against the backdrop of an enormous musical organ onstage, deliberately foregrounding the role of music in the play, which opens with the line, 'If music be the food of love, play on,' as well as providing a visual representation of Olivia's ongoing mourning. The organ was both set piece and working instrument, using sounds recorded from the organ from Holy Trinity Church in Stratford-upon-Avon, where William Shakespeare is buried.

MISTRESS QUICKLY

HENRY IV, PART 1;
HENRY IV, PART 2;
HENRY V AND THE MERRY
WIVES OF WINDSOR

*Everyone's favourite
landlady*

O, THOU HONEY-SEED ROGUE, THOU ART A HONEY-SEED, A MAN-QUELLER, AND A WOMAN-QUELLER.

HENRY IV, PART 2, ACT 2, SCENE 1

MISTRESS QUICKLY

Mistress Quickly is a kind and caring, though usually rather flustered, working-class woman who pops up in four plays. Shakespeare sometimes mocks her – there are definitely jokes made at her expense – but he also allows her wit and honest dignity to shine through. There's some evidence to suggest that her reappearance is partly down to her being popular with audiences, too, which makes sense, as she's a lot of fun.

Her humour is bawdy and knockabout, although she doesn't always realise that what she's saying sounds pretty rude, much to the enjoyment of the audience. She is the unwitting master of the double entendre and also an enthusiastic user of the malapropism – accidently using one word when you mean another, often because you want to appear cleverer than you are. For example, 'he's an infinitive thing upon my score,' she declares of Sir John Falstaff (she was going for 'infinite'), who is 'indited to dinner to the Lubber's-head in Lombard Street'. (For word nerds, the term 'malapropism' wasn't invented at this point – it came into common usage via Mrs Malaprop, a character in a play called *The Rivals*, written nearly 200 years later by Richard Brinsley Sheridan. Shakespeare might have called muddling up your words like this 'acyrologia'.)

Mistress Quickly is slightly different in every play she is in. Shakespeare was more concerned with jokes than continuity, so it's best just to go with it and enjoy her whenever she pops up instead of trying to puzzle out a coherent backstory. Her main role is as part of a sort of unwilling double act with Prince Hal's drinking buddy/dysfunctional father figure, Sir John Falstaff.

She does little or nothing to advance the plot – but she's not there just to be laughed at either.

While the schemes and wars of the aristocratic characters dominate the Henry plays, Mistress Quickly and her associates are just getting on with their lives in Eastcheap, London – getting drunk, falling out, lending each other money. This was much closer to the reality of everyday life for much of the audience watching the plays, and provides welcome light relief from all the battlefield violence and characters who confusingly have the same names.

Perhaps another reason that the 'groundlings' – the audience members who stood up and paid the least to see a play – would have enjoyed Mistress Quickly is that she is a bit of a social climber who wants the Boar's Head Tavern that she runs to be seen as respectable. She emphasises this as often as possible, regardless of evidence to the contrary. The first time we meet her, she is arguing with Falstaff, who (to get out of a debt) is claiming he was robbed in her pub.

> *He hath eaten me out of house and home; he hath put all my substance into that fat belly of his.*
>
> **HENRY IV, PART 2**
> **ACT 2, SCENE 1**

Affronted, she appeals to Prince Hal as adjudicator, saying to Falstaff, 'I am an honest man's wife, and, setting thy knighthood aside, thou art a knave to call me so.' She doesn't really help her cause with the constant swearing, though. She begins many of her lines with the profanity 'O Jesu!' – which was so rude that it was banned on stage a few years after

MISTRESS QUICKLY

WHEN YOUR BOSS LAUNCHES INTO AN ENDLESS PRESENTATION STUFFED WITH MANAGEMENT SPEAK:

Here will be an old abusing of God's patience and the King's English.

WHEN YOU SPOT A GUY YOU USED TO DATE WITH HIS FRIEND WHO YOU NEVER LIKED:

Yonder he comes, and that arrant malmsey-nose Bardolph, with him.

WHEN YOUR FRIEND IS SURPRISINGLY CUTTING ABOUT A MUTUAL ACQUAINTANCE:

By my troth, captain, these are very bitter words.

Shakespeare wrote the Henry histories.

In *Henry IV, Part 2*, not only does Falstaff again owe money to Mistress Quickly, but he has apparently reneged on a promise to marry her (she is evidently now a widow). She produces a comic litany of detail as to when and where this happened in the hope of convincing the Lord Chief Justice of the validity of her case: 'Thou didst swear to me upon a parcel-gilt goblet, sitting in my Dolphin-chamber at the round table, by a sea-coal fire, upon Wednesday in Whitsun week, when the prince broke thy head . . .' and on she goes. However, despite her vexed claim that she is at the end of her tether with Falstaff, having been 'fubbed off, and fubbed off, from this day to that day', her good nature gets the better of her and she is soon lending him even more money.

Mistress Quickly's friend and comic sidekick in *Henry IV, Part 2* is the enjoyably foul-mouthed sex worker Doll Tearsheet. Where Mistress Quickly often finds herself in a verbal muddle, Doll is sharp and fires off witty insults to anyone who gets in her way, resorting to taking out her knife if she thinks the situation demands it. The two squabble and bicker, though their relationship is affectionate. When we first meet Doll, she has a hangover and Mistress Quickly is reassuring her that she doesn't look too bad. At the end of the play, Doll is arrested because she's been involved in a fight. Errant cad Prince Hal is about to be crowned King Henry V and the arrest marks the end of an era for the tavern folk. Falstaff

> *A good heart's worth gold.*
>
> **HENRY IV, PART 2**
> **ACT 2, SCENE 4**

attempts to intervene with the prince but he won't pardon her.

In *Henry V*, the Boar's Head isn't mentioned. Mistress Quickly only makes one appearance – to tell the story of the death of her old sparring partner. Her account of the last moments of Falstaff is touching and comic. It seems fitting that she was present at his demise, but we do hope she managed to get back some of the money he owed her – though it seems unlikely...

> *Marry, this is the short and long of it: you have brought her into such a canaries as 'tis wonderful.*
>
> **THE MERRY WIVES OF WINDSOR ACT 2, SCENE 2**

Some years after Shakespeare finished the Henry plays, he must have been missing the comic antics of Falstaff and Mistress Quickly as he brought them back in a sort of spin-off form in *The Merry Wives of Windsor*. In this bonkers play, Mistress Quickly has a new job as a maid, working for Doctor Caius. Taken away from her East London home of the earlier plays, she's a slightly different character, but no doubt the audience would have been delighted to recognise her from her rude jokes and comic misunderstandings.

Shakespeare was a keen connoisseur of tavern life himself, and we can imagine him looking over his tankard at the women who ran and worked in London's ale houses, Mistress Quickly taking shape in his mind. She was the original soap opera landlady, preceding Peggy Mitchell, Bet Lynch and Angie

Watts, and equally as loved by the public. In the proprietress of the Boar's Head, Shakespeare gives us a timeless character – a lovable and chaotic landlady who does her best to say exactly what's on her mind, even if it gets a little lost in translation. If you have ever accused someone of eating you out of house and home, you're quoting Mistress Quickly. Despite her desire to be seen as respectable, she just can't help being who she is.

RSC STAGE HISTORY

In Gregory Doran's rousing musical version of *Merry Wives* in 2006, Judi Dench played a Mistress Quickly who cartwheeled across the stage (using a body double), then re-emerged from the wings ruffled, to huge applause from the audience. Mistress Quickly was granted a backstory, with Dench singing about a previous love for Falstaff. The show also featured Simon Callow as Sir John Falstaff and impressionist Alistair McGowan as Frank Ford.

GERTRUDE

HAMLET

*Multitasking mother
with a problematic son*

ALL THAT LIVES MUST DIE, PASSING THROUGH NATURE TO ETERNITY

ACT 1, SCENE 2

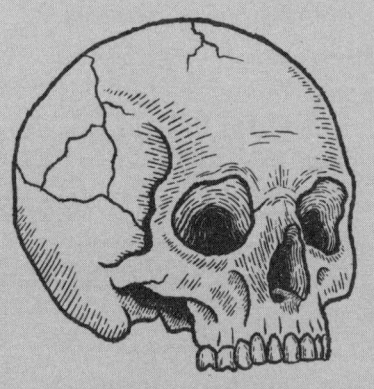

GERTRUDE

As the Queen of Denmark, Gertrude has a lot on her stylish Scandinavian dinner plate. She's intuitive and reads people well, which are important skills when trying to head up a court full of intrigue in a country preparing for possible war with its neighbour, Norway. However, she is at a loss as to what to do about her suddenly rude, aggressive and brooding son.

Of course, if you marry your husband's brother soon after your husband's death, it's going to make family Christmases uncomfortable at the very least. But Gertrude is smart; she would have known this. So why did she do it? Maybe it was political expediency – Hamlet wasn't mature or experienced enough to take over, a queen wasn't seen as strong enough to rule alone and it was the best way to shore up power. Claudius might have manipulated her in order to get his hands on the kingdom, though Gertrude seems too savvy for that. Maybe she'd just always really fancied him.

We don't know. But we do know that Gertrude is trying to be a good mum in the face of some pretty horrible behaviour from her son.

The first time we meet Gertrude, she is attempting to console Hamlet by putting his grief into context: 'Thou know'st 'tis common, all that lives must die, / Passing through nature to eternity.' When everyone else wants to believe that the early signs of the 'madness' Hamlet is feigning are down to his love for Ophelia, Gertrude doesn't buy it: 'I doubt it is no other but the main: / His father's death and our o'erhasty marriage.' So Gertrude is fully aware that she remarried (too) quickly and that her son is not OK with it.

Gertrude likes Ophelia and later says that she wished Hamlet and Ophelia could have married – in direct

WHEN YOU ARE SPENDING TOO MUCH TIME MAKING THE PRESENTATION LOOK NICE AND HAVEN'T ACTUALLY WRITTEN THE SLIDES YET:

More matter, with less art.

THE CLASSIC COMEBACK WHEN YOUR FRIEND KEEPS TELLING YOU THAT THEY REALLY, HONESTLY DON'T FANCY SOMEONE *AT ALL*:

The lady protests too much, methinks.

WHEN YOU'RE TRYING TO REMOVE MOULD FROM THE SHOWER:

I see such black and grainèd spots As will not leave their tinct.

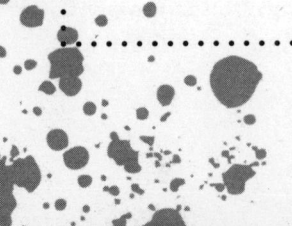

GERTRUDE

contradiction to Laertes's and Polonius's patronising advice to Ophelia, when they told her that Hamlet was too royal for her and out of her league.

We have to assume that Claudius did kill his brother, Old Hamlet, as he pretty much confesses in a soliloquy. Though Shakespeare stops short of confirming it. But does Gertrude know that her new husband was responsible for the death of her old one? Probably not – and there's no suggestion she was complicit either.

There's no question that Hamlet is dealing with a lot. Should he avenge his father's death? Can he be sure the ghost was telling the truth? As otherworldly beings, ghosts can be malevolent forces of darkness, so they aren't necessarily to be trusted. But as Hamlet is wrestling with his dilemma, it is Gertrude (and Ophelia) he takes it out on. Hamlet seems creepily fixated on his mum's sex life. In fact, if anything, judging by how much he brings it up, he is most upset about his mum sleeping with his uncle. Which, although not ideal, you would think would be lower on his 'slings and arrows' list than his father's murder. But not so for Hamlet, who just can't seem to stop picturing them in bed together.

In the 'closet scene', Gertrude is patient and quietly brave when dealing with Hamlet, who has worked himself up to fever pitch and stormed into her bedroom. He forces her to look in a mirror and at a picture of her dead husband, hurling sexual insults at her and breaking off only to kill Polonius, Ophelia's dad, who is idiotically hiding behind a tapestry, eavesdropping. She begs him to stop and is clearly afraid for her own safety, but she holds her nerve and, unable to see the apparition of her former other half who is tormenting Hamlet, tries to understand what has

Thou hast cleft my heart in twain.
ACT 3, SCENE 4

caused her son to behave in this way. She says, 'O gentle son, / Upon the heat and flame of thy distemper / Sprinkle cool patience' – perhaps the Elizabethan parenting equivalent of 'Take a breath and tell me about these big feelings you're having, darling.'

Gertrude's death in Act 5 comes because she drinks from a cup of wine that Claudius has poisoned, in case the poisoned sword in the fencing duel between Hamlet and Laertes at the finale wasn't poisoned enough to kill Hamlet. Guys, accidents were bound to happen. At least we know that Gertrude wasn't aware that her husband was planning on killing her son, as presumably she would have been more careful otherwise.

Gertrude doesn't get much airtime in *Hamlet* – she gets a paltry 4 per cent of the play's lines. We hear much more about her from her angry son than we do directly from her – and Hamlet's anger reveals more about himself than it does about Gertrude. As an older woman with higher status, Gertrude has more freedom and agency than Ophelia, but, despite being queen, she is still severely limited by the stifling rules and conventions of the court. Even her death is overshadowed by men swinging their egos around. Oh, Hamlet, if only you could have just sat down and had a proper chat with your mum, she might have known what to do and all of this could have been sorted out over a cuppa. Gertrude was a smart lady who cared about her son and really wanted to understand.

RSC STAGE HISTORY

In 1958 Coral Browne played Gertrude at the Shakespeare Memorial Theatre, opposite Michael Redgrave as Hamlet. As part of the tour to Moscow, the cast had an unexpected visitor backstage: the Cambridge spy and Soviet double-agent Guy Burgess. He was drunkenly sick in Redgrave's dressing room but befriended Browne, who later sent him eight suits from her tailor in London. This bizarre incident was made into a 1983 BBC television play entitled *An Englishman Abroad*, written by Alan Bennett, with Browne playing herself. The episode was also the basis of Bennett's double bill of plays, *Single Spies*.

TITANIA

A MIDSUMMER NIGHT'S DREAM

Fairy escapes controlling husband for one night with lovely donkey

I AM A SPIRIT OF NO COMMON RATE.

ACT 3, SCENE 1

TITANIA

Regal, stubborn, otherworldly and powerful, Titania is the queen of the fairies, *A Midsummer Night's Dream*'s magical beings whose mischief is behind the events of the play. However, she too is subjected to the same magic potion cooked up by Puck that Lysander and Demetrius are dosed with. Even fairies can't escape the irrational, illogical nature of love, it seems.

We first meet Titania in the middle of an ongoing row with her husband, Oberon, the fairy king. These two have a pretty tempestuous relationship – literally: such is their power that when they are fighting, it causes weird stuff to happen in the natural world. The seasons are all out of whack and there have been rains and floods. *Well, that's your fault,* says Oberon, refusing to accept his share of responsibility.

There's a strong streak of jealousy running through this relationship. Titania accuses Oberon of flirting with mortal women in disguise. *Why are you here? It's surely not to bless the marriage between Theseus and Hippolyta?* she asks tauntingly – it seems that Oberon and Hippolyta once had a 'thing'. *Well, you fancy Theseus!* Oberon shoots back. Do these two really care about monogamy, we wonder, or is this the erotic spark that keeps things fresh?

Their current row – on the surface, at least – is about a 'changeling' who Titania has adopted after his mother, a mortal, died. Oberon wants Titania to hand over the boy so he can become part of his fairy retinue. But – as any good marriage counsellor would ask Oberon straight away – what is this *really* about? Titania clearly had a very affectionate relationship with the child's mother, and she promised she would bring him up.

> *Never since the middle summer's spring*
> *Met we on hill, in dale, forest or mead,*
> *By pavèd fountain or by rushy brook,*
> *Or in the beachèd margent of the sea.*
>
> **ACT 2, SCENE 1**

So what is Oberon's problem?

Titania is independent and powerful, while Oberon seems like quite a needy fairy who doesn't like it if his wife shows affection elsewhere. Titania is strong enough that she is usually impervious to his controlling behaviour and well able to draw boundaries. In a gesture of peace, she asks Oberon to join the dance at the upcoming wedding (fairies love a wedding and would often invite themselves along, according to folk beliefs at the time), but if he won't behave himself, he should leave her alone. Still, Oberon won't let the issue of the changeling boy go, and so Titania simply leaves, unbothered by his anger.

Oberon is suffering a serious case of wounded male pride and not-getting-his-own-way-itis. It's all Titania's fault, he decides, and he's going to 'torment thee for this injury'. Having come up with an idea, he immediately outsources it – 'My gentle Puck, come hither.' It seems a bit weird that the trick Oberon wants to play involves getting Titania, his wife, to fall in love with someone else, however conventionally unsuitable, but perhaps, like the jealousy thing, it's just what this couple are into.

Under the spell of a love potion, Titania falls for Bottom, who has been given the head of an ass by

TITANIA

WHEN YOU WAKE UP CONFUSED ON THE SOFA:

Tell me how it came this night That I sleeping here was found.

WHEN EVERYONE HAS THE SAME WINTER COLD:

Rheumatic diseases do abound.

WHEN A ROW ERUPTS OVER AN OTHERWISE FRIENDLY BOARD GAME:

With thy brawls thou hast disturbed our sport.

Puck. Bottom is, admittedly, not the sharpest stick in the forest, but he's not an idiot – 'reason and love keep little company together nowadays,' he says, entirely accurately. And the two are very sweet together. Titania kisses his furry ears and says romantically, 'Sleep thou, and I will wind thee in my arms.' Bottom – having been told that his new fairy attendants can bring him jewels – asks only for a face scratch and some oats. While Titania is under the spell, she agrees to give up the changeling that she is so fond of, just as Oberon planned.

Titania is a strong, wise and loyal fairy queen – is she really into childish, controlling Oberon? Perhaps she can see past his petty behaviour to his redeeming features (his meddling in Helena's love life came from a good place, sort of, and he does go on to bless the marriage of his possible ex, Hippolyta). Or maybe fairy Tinder has very limited options. When cured of her enchantment, Titania claims Bottom's donkey face gives her the ick – 'O, how mine eyes do loathe his visage now!' But even when she's flirting with an ass, there's still something majestic and sexy about Titania that Oberon's prank is unable to undermine. Oberon gets what he wants – but only through the kind of trickery that Titania would see as beneath her. Once the spell is lifted, Titania will return to being as powerful and independent as she was at the start. Oberon will have to deal with that, or maybe Titania will start to think back fondly on her one night of passion with good-hearted Bottom . . .

RSC STAGE HISTORY

Josette Simon doubled up her queenly duties in Michael Boyd's erotic *A Midsummer Night's Dream* in 1999, playing both Titania, queen of the fairies, and Hippolyta, queen of the Amazons, opposite Nicholas Jones's Oberon and Theseus. The *Independent* called them 'the sexiest, most commanding Oberon and Titania of recent years.'

VOLUMNIA

CORIOLANUS

Mother always knows best

THY VALIANTNESS WAS MINE, THOU SUCK'ST IT FROM ME, BUT OWE THY PRIDE THYSELF.

ACT 3, SCENE 2

VOLUMNIA

Perhaps the original tiger mum, Volumnia is very, very invested in her son's success. This would be bad enough if her son's ambitions were to be an actor or play football professionally, but Coriolanus's chosen field is war. He is very into fighting. And Volumnia is very into living vicariously through him.

Volumnia sent her only son – real name Caius Martius – to fight in his first battle when he was still in his teens. We don't get the sense that there was much emotional connection or talking about your feelings in their household when little Caius was growing up, to put it mildly. We don't know what happened to his dad, he is never mentioned; it's like Coriolanus is Volumnia's creation – she has shaped him into the warrior he is through the power of her will. She dominates him and revels in his successes on the battlefield.

The elephant in the room is that their relationship ... maybe crosses some boundaries. The language Volumnia uses when talking about her son is occasionally somewhat sexual. Her second line in the entire play is to Coriolanus's wife, Virgilia: 'If my son were my husband, I should freelier rejoice in that absence wherein he won honour than in the embracements of his bed where he would show most love.' Er, why are you thinking of him in terms of a husband and imagining him in bed?

She also knows exactly how many scars from war wounds he has on his body and is excited to hear that he has acquired two more from his latest adventures. He arrives home and she rabidly fangirls him. He has pretty much taken the city of Corioles singlehandedly, hence his new name, 'Coriolanus'. He's now in line for a

SHAKESPEARE'S STRONG WOMEN

WHEN YOUR HOUSEMATE IS IN A BAD MOOD AND NEEDS SOME ALONE TIME:

Let her alone, lady: as she is now, she will but disease our better mirth.

WHEN YOUR KIDS COMPLAIN ABOUT BEING TOLD TO TURN OFF THE XBOX EVEN THOUGH IT'S BEDTIME ON A SCHOOL NIGHT:

*Say my request's unjust,
And spurn me back: but if it be not so,
Thou art not honest,
and the gods will plague thee
That thou restrain'st from
me the duty which
To a mother's part belongs.*

FAKE IT TILL YOU MAKE IT:

*Action is eloquence,
and the eyes of th' ignorant
More learnèd than the ears.*

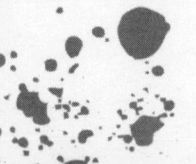

VOLUMNIA

new job as a consul, a powerful city official, as a reward. Volumnia really wants him to get it.

The issue is that he will have to go in front of the citizens of Rome, show off his battle wounds and act grateful. This makes him feel uncomfortable as 'being humble' isn't really in his wheelhouse. As can happen when someone is promoted to management on the strength of their work achievements, he doesn't have the people skills for a leadership role.

At first, it seems to work, but then the people turn against him. It's a febrile time anyway, with riots threatened over food shortages. And Coriolanus doesn't believe in democracy; he's an aristocratic snob who thinks ordinary people are idiots who shouldn't get a say – a view, he says, that he got from his mother. Volumnia might agree with the sentiment, but she is smarter than him and – showing herself to be an excellent spin doctor – convinces him to pretend to be what the people want him to be. He agrees, but very sulkily.

However, it all goes wrong and recalcitrant Coriolanus is expelled from Rome. Volumnia is absolutely furious and gives Brutus and Sicinius, two officials who have been working against her son, a large and loud piece of her mind. They are, quite rightly, terrified. Coriolanus seeks out his former enemy, Aufidius, who has a lot of respect for him, and together they decide to attack Rome. Hearing about this, some emissaries try to talk him out of it. Aufidius is a brilliant soldier, after all, and Rome has got enough problems as it is without being under siege from a socially clumsy war veteran. Everyone's arguments and pleas fail, though, so there is only one thing for it: send in Volumnia.

You can be as much of a badass soldier as you like, but you still have to answer to your mum, Coriolanus finds out. 'There's no man in the world / More bound to 's mother,' she says – that's taken as read – but she still seems worried she won't be able to convince him. So she throws herself into her argument, appealing to him on the grounds of family, patriotism, honour and anything else she can think of. She equates herself with Rome: she is speaking on behalf of the state, but, more than that, she *is* the city. If he attacks Rome, he is attacking her – the single most important thing in his life. And she cleverly frames changing his mind as a victory rather than a defeat. It's a speech of rhetorical brilliance and it works.

Volumnia is now celebrated as the hero who has saved Rome, just as her son was at the beginning of the play. 'This Volumnia / Is worth of consuls, senators, patricians,' says Menenius, who had himself failed to convince Coriolanus. 'Behold our patroness, the life of Rome!' shouts an excited senator.

But in changing his mind, Coriolanus has signed his own death warrant. Aufidius orchestrates his death for going back on his word. Coriolanus knew what would happen when he agreed to his mum's demands. Did Volumnia suspect this outcome, too? It seems likely, as she is smart and understands the intricacies of war and politics. Did she choose her love for her city over her love for her son? Maybe she never really saw him as a real person in his own right. He was more an instrument she created to bring glory and honour to herself.

We don't know how she reacts to her son's death, as Shakespeare doesn't bring Volumnia back to the stage. Nonetheless, she is one of Shakespeare's most majestic and authoritative female characters. Just by being herself, she overturns prevailing, traditional ideas of subservient femininity – but no one challenges her for this. The power of her mind and her eloquent speech are what save Rome, rather than a sword – along with a hefty dose of maternal manipulation. Poor Coriolanus never stood a chance.

RSC STAGE HISTORY

Margaret Tyzack's powerful performance of Volumnia in 1972–73 conveyed both strength and vulnerability – described by critics as 'a towering, terrifying tigress fighting for her son's life'. Her role was commemorated in a cartoon in *Punch* magazine, where she is shown berating her son Coriolanus, played by Nicol Williamson for the London run at the Aldwych Theatre.

VIOLA

TWELFTH NIGHT

Shipwreck survivor drags up and falls in love with boss

THEN THINK YOU RIGHT: I AM NOT WHAT I AM.

ACT 3, SCENE 1

VIOLA

When we first meet Viola, she has just found herself in a strange land where she doesn't know anyone. She has been separated from her twin brother after a shipwreck, and although the sailors who rescued her say encouraging things about having seen him clinging onto a mast, she has no idea if he is alive or dead. She immediately decides that, rather than throw herself on the mercy of strangers, she will disguise herself until she figures out what she wants to do. Viola is no helpless heroine – she is going to take charge of her own destiny. And to do so, she will dress as a man.

So begins this wonderful comedy of gender fluidity and sexual ambiguity. *Twelfth Night* famously revolves around mistaken identity and love triangles, but it's Viola's self-belief and charisma that get the action going. She makes a plan and doesn't doubt for a minute that she can pull it off. And this confidence convinces and captivates everyone around her.

Viola tells the sailors she's going to get a job with a local duke, Orsino. And not only does he take her on as a page – believing she is a boy called Cesario – but within three days he seems to trust her completely, explaining that he has 'unclasped / To thee the book even of my secret soul'. Which has clearly had a major effect on Viola, as, in the same short timeframe, she has fallen in love with the duke.

She's in a bit of a pickle and she knows it. Not least because Orsino wants her to go to Olivia, with whom he is infatuated, to see if she can convince her to marry him. The self-indulgent, emotionally incontinent duke has been dramatically pining for Olivia for a while, but all the other messengers he's sent have had the door firmly closed in their faces. Orsino reckons Cesario is the 'man' for the job.

Despite her feelings for Orsino, Viola does visit Olivia and makes as strong an impression on her as she seems to have on everyone else. Olivia tells her in no uncertain terms that she's not going to marry Orsino — presumably much to Viola's relief, though perhaps less so when it dawns on her that Olivia has fallen for the 'brazen' Cesario. Which means Viola is now in an even bigger pickle.

Later, Viola, as Cesario, tries to make the duke see he's being ridiculous. This is not love — he barely knows Olivia and he's wallowing in a kind of romantic self-pity. Viola somehow manages to stop herself from shouting, 'She's just not into you!' in his face and, ever practical and with probably more compassion than he deserves, tries to get him to see reason. The duke argues that women aren't capable of the all-consuming 'love' he feels — there is 'no woman's heart / So big, to hold so much. They lack retention.' Viola, internally rolling her eyes, responds by trying to tell him that real love is about what you do — it's not grandstanding statements and getting your musicians to play the same song over and over. 'My father had a daughter loved a man,' she says. 'As it might be, perhaps, were I a woman, / I should your lordship.' She makes it pretty obvious, but Orsino is oblivious to the subtext. Tellingly, he asks whether this 'sister' died from her unrequited love — not something we can imagine Viola ever doing, whose love for Orsino is patient and underpinned by care for him.

> *This fellow is wise enough to play the fool, And to do that well craves a kind of wit.*
>
> **ACT 3, SCENE 1**

VIOLA

WHEN YOU TAKE THE PERFECT SELFIE:

Most radiant, exquisite and unmatchable beauty.

WHEN YOU ARE ABOUT TO BUTTER SOMEONE UP TO GET WHAT YOU WANT:

I will on with my speech in your praise, and then show you the heart of my message.

WHEN SOMEONE ASKS ABOUT WHAT YOU DID AT UNI:

I can say little more than I have studied, and that question's out of my part.

Meanwhile, Sebastian, Viola's twin, has survived the shipwreck and is making his way to Illyria. After much confusion, his appearance untangles the whole complicated knot and the siblings are thrilled to be reunited. Viola explains who she really is and Orsino finally gets what Viola has been trying to tell him – 'Boy, thou hast said to me a thousand times / Thou never shouldst love woman like to me.' The love triangle is resolved as Viola marries Orsino, and Sebastian – the spitting image of Cesario – marries Olivia.

Does Orsino shift his love rather quickly? Well, yes, but this is a comedy, after all. Viola has seen something honest, open and true in the duke. When he thinks he has lost Olivia to Cesario, Orsino first threatens to take him away from her, but then relents and asks them to go away somewhere so he won't have to see them together. Which, in the context of Shakespeare's plays, which are riddled with highly emotional men threatening revenge when they don't get what they want, is a pretty magnanimous response. We can believe that the time Viola and Orsino have spent together as friends has allowed them to get to know one another in a way that they couldn't have had Orsino known Viola was a woman from the start, thanks to the gendered social order of the day.

She might not have set out to fall in love, but in choosing to take her own unconventional path, our resourceful, can-do heroine ultimately gets what she wants and on her own terms – brother, husband and (hot) new sister-in-law. The play rewards her for her bravery and self-belief far more than for her beauty and feminine charm. Maybe now Orsino's long-suffering musicians can get a day off . . .

RSC STAGE HISTORY

Dinita Gohil played Viola in Christopher Luscombe's lavish production of *Twelfth Night* in 2017. Designer Simon Higlett's Victorian sets reflected Queen Victoria's own mourning period for Albert, as well as highlighting the problematic nature of the cross-gender relationships – homosexuality in the era was illegal, making the love triangle between Viola, Olivia and Orsino all the more dangerous. Orsino (Nicholas Bishop) lounged in a dressing gown in his Oscar Wildean home, painting partially-clothed male models, with Gohil as his doting, wide-eyed aide.

DESDEMONA

OTHELLO

Never trust a soldier

HIS UNKINDNESS MAY DEFEAT MY LIFE, BUT NEVER TAINT MY LOVE.

ACT 4, SCENE 2

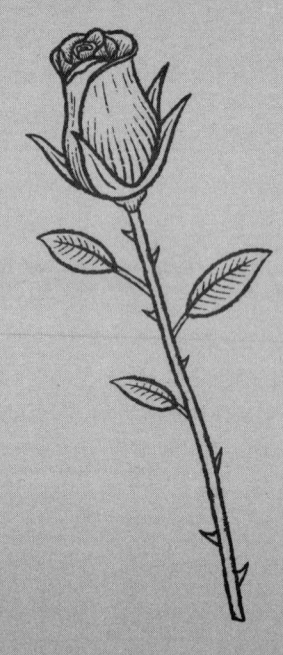

DESDEMONA

> *Before exploring the character of Desdemona, we must first acknowledge that for some critical race scholars,* Othello *is an irredeemable play that shouldn't be performed anymore. Scholars point to a vilifying of Black masculinity inherent in the text, stating that the play represents a fantasy of Black masculinity. This viewpoint needs careful consideration alongside any critique of the female characters in the play.*

While she is sometimes portrayed as a naive, docile pawn in the game of a nasty, jealous man, there is a lot more to Desdemona. She is honest, brave and empathetic. Her loyalty may be misplaced and manipulated, but she is no fool – rather something of an idealist who is thrown into a world where she doesn't understand the rules.

Brabantio is incensed that Othello – a Venetian soldier and Black man – has dared marry his daughter in secret. *My sweet little girl would never do such a thing!* he complains to his buddies at the senate, which suggests that he doesn't know her very well, as she clearly has. Desdemona explains that she fell for Othello because of his amazing life story and she wanted him as much as he wanted her. She calmly tells her father that her loyalty now lies with her husband, just as her mother's loyalty was to him on marriage.

Othello appeals to her adventurous spirit; she wants to accompany him to war – there's a battle brewing between the Turks and the Venetians in Cyprus, and the Venetians need Othello, one of their best soldiers, over there. 'O my fair warrior!' Othello greets Desdemona

WHEN TWO FRIENDS' BIRTHDAY DRINKS CLASH:

I do perceive here a divided duty.

WHEN YOUR COLLEAGUE IS STUCK ON MUTE ON THE ZOOM CALL:

Alas, she has no speech.

WHEN YOU ARE WORRIED YOU HAVE PUT YOUR FOOT IN IT:

Alas, what ignorant sin have I committed?

when they reunite in Cyprus, having travelled there separately. 'Our great captain's captain,' Cassio calls her, highlighting how enamoured Othello is by her and hinting at her inner strength. So what goes wrong?

Well, Iago, of course. He's famously out to get Othello for no good reason other than he passed him up for a promotion and he suspects Othello slept with his wife, Emilia. Or so he says. But he's more than happy – literally quite delighted – to drag anyone into his scheme. Terrifyingly, he is able to get everyone to trust him. He convinces Othello that Desdemona is having an affair with the gallant, handsome, soldier Cassio. And he persuades Desdemona to 'help' Cassio after he's demoted following a drunken fight that Iago engineered.

The main destructive force in the play is the jealousy that consumes Othello. But there are other things that create the right conditions. Desdemona seems out of her depth in Cyprus. She fell in love with her hero soldier without really understanding his world, which is violent and full of male egos. As he was charming her with eloquent tales of his background – his lucky escapes, his travels, his rise from slave to military man – she didn't really make the connection that he has been through a lot (including everyone constantly calling him 'Moor' and racially discriminating against him). He has some baggage, which Iago exploits, knowing which buttons to press. Desdemona – and we the audience – can only look on as Othello gets angrier and angrier and treats his wife increasingly badly.

The other problem, as is so often the case, is Desdemona's sexuality (which Iago is creepily obsessed with). She seems comfortable with slightly racy conversations – her banter with Iago on the dockside in Cyprus shows she's not shocked by rude jokes. 'These are old fond paradoxes to make fools laugh i' th' ale-house,' she breezily tells him. Plus, she is not obedient and docile. She has her own opinions and tries to convince her husband of them. She is beautiful and Othello is physically attracted to her, but that means other men will be, too, which is at the root of his growing paranoia. Is Desdemona a bit of a flirt? Some interpretations say she is, but there's also a strong argument to be made that this is simply her natural exuberance and good humour.

Before Othello, driven mad by jealousy, comes in to kill her, Desdemona seems to have an idea of what is going to happen, asking her attendant, Emilia (see page 264), Iago's abused wife, to put her marriage sheets on the bed and use them for her shroud should she die.

Desdemona begs for her life while Othello smothers her, but is she resigned to her fate? When Desdemona briefly comes round after Emilia enters the room and asks her who has done this terrible thing (Shakespeare had clearly not seen enough crime shows to know that's not how suffocation works), her last lines before she dies are: 'Nobody: I myself. Farewell. / Commend me to my kind lord. O, farewell!' She forgives Othello with her dying breath. Is this Shakespeare asking us to forgive him, too? Is it Desdemona's words that turn him from murdering psychopath to tragic hero?

We know that the only untruth Desdemona told was about the hanky that Emilia took under pressure from Iago. It was Othello's first gift to her, and it becomes a focus for his obsession with her fidelity. Under pressure from Othello, Desdemona claims she hasn't lost it when she knows it is missing in an attempt to de-escalate his rage. This tiny lie serves to highlight how honest and true she is, in contrast with Othello's wild suspicions.

Desdemona is not a naive girl, she is a passionate woman who is so certain of her love for Othello that she can't comprehend why he doubts her fidelity. She trusts the wrong people because of her goodness and – whatever we might think of it – is loyal to the last.

RSC STAGE HISTORY

Mary Ure played Desdemona in Tony Richardson's 1959 production, opposite Paul Robeson who was playing Othello for the third time, with Sam Wanamaker (who later reconstructed Shakespeare's Globe Theatre) as Iago. Ure had previously been directed by Tony Richardson in the film of John Osborne's *Look Back in Anger*, which was released in the same year as the production.

PAULINA

THE WINTER'S TALE

Powerful force of nature is not to be messed with

IT IS AN HERETIC THAT MAKES THE FIRE, NOT SHE WHICH BURNS IN'T.

ACT 2, SCENE 3

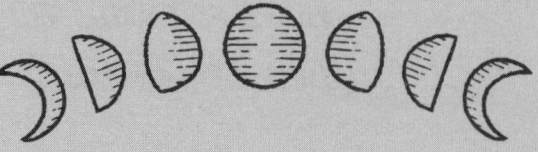

PAULINA

The *Winter's Tale* is a weird play. It mixes elements of tragedy and comedy, shifts between places and times, and ends with a plot twist – which is highly unusual in Shakespeare's plays, as usually the audience is in on all the characters' secrets. But at the heart of the play, pulling a lot of the strings, is Paulina, perhaps the original exasperated middle-aged woman with zero effs left to give.

Paulina's best friend is Hermione, who is married to Leontes, King of Sicilia. Leontes's best friend is Polixenes, the King of Bohemia. Polixenes has been visiting the Sicilian court and Leontes doesn't want him to go home, so Hermione, ever the dutiful wife, convinces him to stay a bit longer to make her husband happy. Is Leontes pleased and grateful? No. He accuses his wife of having an affair with his friend and throws her in prison – even though she is pregnant with his child.

Paulina is outraged. First, she goes to see Hermione in prison, wielding her natural authority so that the jailer lets her in. She can't see the queen but speaks to her attendant, Emilia, who tells her the queen has given birth to a baby girl. Even though she thinks that the king seems both mad and dangerous, Paulina decides she's going to take the baby to him and hope he softens when he meets his daughter. She's not going to try to sweet talk him either – she's going to let him have a piece of her mind. 'There is no lady living / So meet for this great errand,' says Emilia admiringly. *Er, I'm not sure you're allowed to take the baby,* says the jailer. *Don't worry about that,* replies Paulina, *I'll make sure you don't get into trouble.* We could all do with a righteous Paulina turning up if ever

WHEN YOUR FRIEND IS REFUSING
TO GET DRESSED AND LEAVE THE HOUSE
AFTER A BAD BREAK-UP:

Good lady,
No court in Europe is
too good for thee.
What dost thou then in prison?

WHAT YOU'D LIKE TO SAY TO YOUR EX:

Will you swear
Never to marry but
by my free leave?

WHEN YOU RESCUE SOMEONE
FROM A SPIDER:

Do not you fear.
Upon mine honour, I
Will stand betwixt
you and danger.

PAULINA

we find ourselves in prison, wrongly accused.

Paulina marches straight in to see the king, even though one of his lords and her husband, Antigonus, try to stop her. *I knew she'd turn up here*, says Leontes. *Can't you control your wife?* he asks. Antigonus admits that no, actually, he can't. He makes a lame joke about her being like a wilful horse, but also says he trusts that she knows what's right.

However, the plan backfires. Leontes refuses to believe the baby is his, even as Paulina points out how much she looks like him. Paulina tells him what she thinks of him – in fact, here is a woman who seems incapable of not speaking her mind, even to a powerful man who could order her death. Leontes calls her names, and she shoots back that he has no proof of his wife's infidelity other than his 'weak-hinged fancy'. But there's nothing to be done other than try to save the baby's life. *Burn her!* says Leontes, shockingly. Antigonus protests and the king changes his order – to abandon her in 'some remote and desert place quite out / Of our dominions'.

Shortly after, Mamillius, the king's young son, dies, and so does Hermione, collapsing at her trial when she

> *What studied torments,*
> *tyrant, hast for me?*
> *What wheels? Racks? Fires?*
> *What flaying? Boiling?*
> *In leads or oils? What old or*
> *newer torture*
> *Must I receive, whose every*
> *word deserves*
> *To taste of thy most worst?*
>
> **ACT 3, SCENE 2**

hears this news. Antigonus dies, too – at the hands of a bear when depositing the baby on a beach as per a dream he had. The stage direction 'Exit, pursued by a bear' is probably better known than the plot of the play itself, making Paulina's husband's death strangely comic – and also providing a headache for theatre directors for hundreds of years.

So Leontes has destroyed his family and it's only the end of Act 3. Plenty of men in Shakespeare's plays hurt those closest to them through their arrogance and refusal to listen (see: King Lear, Lord Capulet, Titus Andronicus, among others), but few get the chance to dwell on their mistakes and possibly make amends. Which is one of the reasons why *The Winter's Tale* is so interesting.

The other main reason is Paulina. She is slightly ridiculed in the play for being an interfering battleaxe – a bit of a Karen, maybe – but she's seriously impressive. While other Shakespearean heroines have to pretend to be men to get any kind of influence or authority, Paulina just takes it for herself. From her first line on arrival at the jail – 'The keeper of the prison, call to him. / Let him have knowledge who I am' – she shows a powerful confidence and sense of self.

For all of his anger and desire to exert patriarchal control, Leontes doesn't quite know what to make of her. At one point, he calls her a 'mankind witch'. Witches are usually female, of

> *If I prove honey-mouthed, let my tongue blister And never to my red-looked anger be The trumpet any more.*
>
> **ACT 2, SCENE 2**

course, but he's flummoxed by her alpha energy. To accuse a woman of being like a man should be an insult at this time – women are meant to be soft, kind and subservient – but it's also paradoxically a compliment. Paulina is strong enough to hold her ground and stand up to the king.

The ending of *The Winter's Tale* is much more in keeping with a comedy, or the era's 'romance' plays, than the tragedy elements at the start. And the most surprising part of the denouement, the twist the audience don't know about, is all Paulina.

Leontes and Hermione's daughter survived her abandonment. In Act 4, it's sixteen years later and Perdita, as she is now known, wants to marry Florizel, the son of Leontes's estranged friend Polixenes. But she can't, says Polixenes, because she's the daughter of a shepherd. The couple run away to Sicilia where Leontes – who has quite rightly been feeling guilty this whole time – welcomes Florizel. Polixenes turns up in hot pursuit, Leontes makes it up with him and realises Perdita is his daughter. A princess! So she can marry Florizel, after all. Strangely, Perdita never asks her dad, *So, sorry, what happened to my mother?*

> *All faults I make, when I shall come to know them, I do repent.*
> **ACT 3, SCENE 2**

But then comes Paulina's big reveal. She's been campaigning against Leontes remarrying and never hesitates to remind him of what he did. Though he seems to accept that now, and values Paulina – 'O grave and good Paulina, the great comfort / That

I have had of thee!' Paulina has had a statue of poor Hermione made and everyone is going to its unveiling. Much to their surprise, the statue comes to life. It *is* Hermione.

How does Paulina do it? Did she fake Hermione's death and hide her in 'that removed house' that Paulina, we're told in passing, visits a couple of times a day? (And if so, why did Hermione not just run away and enjoy life away from her madly jealous husband?) Or did Hermione really die and Paulina has somehow brought her back to life? Is she a 'mankind witch' after all? No one asks any difficult questions, and we are left none the wiser, but Paulina gets a new husband out of it, Camillo, and it seems like everyone will live weirdly happily ever after, with Leontes having the chance to right all those wrongs. Let's hope Paulina's new husband has the sense to stay away from bears.

RSC STAGE HISTORY

Noma Dumezweni played a fearless Paulina in David Farr's 2009 production, which was revived for a 2011 New York transfer. Upon reading the part, she thought, 'Oh my God, I want to meet this woman! She is life, she is family, she is loyalty, she is courage, she sees the people she loves and she challenges them.' Designer Jon Bausor set Sicilia in a library, the tall shelves of books falling upon Leontes as he descended into grief at the loss of his son and wife. The torn pages from the books were then transformed into a huge puppet paper bear in Bohemia for the infamous 'Exit, pursued by a bear' stage direction.

PORTIA

THE MERCHANT OF VENICE

Gameshow prize turned hotshot lawyer

I'LL PROVE THE PRETTIER FELLOW OF THE TWO, AND WEAR MY DAGGER WITH THE BRAVER GRACE.

ACT 3, SCENE 4

> *Before we look at daughters and dads through the tribulations of Portia, we should acknowledge that* The Merchant of Venice *is a problematic text – specifically in terms of the antisemitic tropes it can perpetuate (depending on interpretation). Any discussion about the play and its merits must grapple honestly with that legacy.*

Dads cause so many problems in Shakespeare's plays. No matter how smart and capable their daughters are, they can't resist sticking their oar in. And even though he is dead, Portia's dad is no exception, trying to control who she marries from beyond the grave.

Presumably a fan of gameshows, Portia's father has stipulated in his will that her potential suitors must choose from between three caskets: gold, silver and lead. If they pick the right box, they can marry her – whether she wants to marry them or not. Portia is understandably not happy about this situation: 'I may neither choose whom I would nor refuse whom I dislike, so is the will of a living daughter curbed by the will of a dead father.'

In a scene that will be familiar to anyone who has ever gossiped about guys with their girlfriends, Portia discusses the potential suitors/contestants with her best friend, Nerissa, dispensing hilarious and observant judgements on all of them. The Neapolitan prince is obsessed with horses and weirdly proud that he knows how to shoe them ('I am much afraid my lady his mother played false with a smith'). The English baron is oddly dressed and she can't understand a word he says, as, being English, he has failed to learn any other languages. The Count Palatine never smiles ('I fear he will prove the weeping philosopher when he grows old, being so full of unmannerly sadness in his youth'), while the Duke of Saxony's nephew is horrible when sober and worse when drunk. Portia suggests they 'set a deep glass of Rhenish wine on the contrary casket' to make sure he definitely picks that one. However, if no one ever chooses the right box, then Portia is worried she will 'die as chaste as Diana'. Would she prefer to be single or put up with a substandard guy?

> *O, me, the word 'choose'!*
> *I may neither choose whom I would, nor refuse whom I dislike, so is the will of a living daughter curbed by the will of a dead father.*
>
> **ACT 1, SCENE 2**

Nerissa claims to have faith that Portia's 'ever virtuous' dad knew what he was doing – or maybe she is just trying to reassure her friend. But it's still hard to understand why, when he had such an insightful daughter, who clearly doesn't suffer fools, he felt the need to come up with this silly game.

And yet, by luck or some sort of divine intervention, it does work out. Following a few more encounters with potential husbands who fail to figure it out, Portia's preferred candidate turns up to have a go. She tries to dissuade Bassanio from choosing a casket straight away, as that means they can hang out for a bit longer. But he can't stand the suspense. 'I am locked in one of them. / If you do love me, you will find me out,' Portia says, tellingly. Fortunately, Bassanio chooses the unadorned lead box and discovers a picture of Portia inside, confirming that he has won this week's star prize.

Great. All wrapped up then. That was easy. Except, right at that moment, Bassanio's friends turn up to tell him that his best friend, Antonio, is in a lot of trouble. Having just delivered a speech explaining how everything she has is now Bassiano's and how happy she is that her 'gentle spirit' will now be 'directed' by her soon-to-be husband, Portia immediately takes charge. They will go to the church and get married, then Bassiano will go sort out the problem with his friend (using Portia's money) and come back straight away. *Are you sure that's OK?* Bassanio asks, deferentially.

Except the problem is not that easy to solve. Antonio – the titular merchant of Venice – borrowed money from the lender Shylock on Bassanio's behalf so he could go to Belmont and play marriage Deal or No Deal. In a stroke of amazingly horrible luck, all Antonio's ships simultaneously sank in different parts of the world and he defaulted on his debt. Unfortunately, Shylock, a victim of ongoing antisemitism, which is challenging for modern audiences, has just been robbed by his daughter and is out for revenge. He wants to call in the gruesome penalty for non-repayment – a pound

How far that little candle throws his beams! So shines a good deed in a naughty world.
ACT 5, SCENE 1

WHEN HE'S HOT BUT HAS LITERALLY NO CHAT:

He is a proper man's picture, but alas, who can converse with a dumb show?

WHEN A COLLEAGUE ASKS YOU TO SPONSOR THEM FOR THEIR SEVENTH 5K OF THE YEAR:

'Twere good you do so much for charity.

WHEN YOU'RE BABYSITTING YOUR FRIEND'S SQUABBLING CHILDREN:

A quarrel, ho, already? What's the matter?

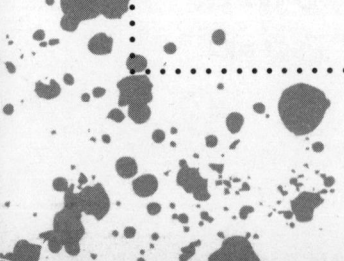

of Antonio's flesh.

Portia decides she's going to save the day, disguising herself as a male lawyer to fight against Shylock's bond in court. It's certainly

> *How many things by season seasoned are To their right praise and true perfection!*
>
> **ACT 5, SCENE 1**

brave of her to go to the defence of a man she has never met in such a risky way. We get a sense before she leaves for Venice that she is relishing the idea of grabbing hold of this freedom, particularly having been subject to her father's tiresome terms and conditions regarding her marriage for so long. She jokes to Nerissa that she's going to act like 'a fine bragging youth' – 'I have within my mind / A thousand raw tricks of these bragging Jacks / Which I will practise.' Presumably she's learned these 'tricks' from some of the hopeless suitors who wanted to marry her.

In court, Portia successfully argues that Shylock may be contractually entitled to a pound of Antonio's flesh, which he insists on having, but in gaining this, he must not spill a drop of his blood. Which is obviously impossible. The duke presiding over the case finds in her favour and decides Shylock must forfeit half of his estate and convert to Christianity.

So, it's a happy ending, right? The play is, after all, classified as a comedy. Portia gets her man, Nerissa gets her man, Jessica gets her man, Antonio's life is saved and his debt wiped clean. But Shylock has to surrender his loan, give up half of his property and change religion? The play is problematic, and despite famously questioning and challenging prejudices of the era in Shylock's 'Hath not a Jew eyes?' speech, its antisemitic undercurrent is troubling today.

Modern readings of the play view Portia as a privileged woman who condemns someone with less privilege, with a harsh judgement. She doesn't seem to recognise that Shylock has been subject to persecution not wholly dissimilar to the restrictions and prejudices she has suffered because she's a woman. Portia is a layered character who shows herself to be intelligent, courageous and resourceful, but she is also fortunate in her wealth and social standing in Belmont. She's a tricky character to play today because she is both kind and cruel, friend and foe. She's a complicated woman in a complicated world.

RSC STAGE HISTORY

Rupert Goold's 2010 production was set in a glitzy Las Vegas casino, complete with fruit machines and roulette tables and the servant Lancelot Gobbo as an Elvis impersonator. Patrick Stewart was the prosperous casino owner who intimidated his daughter and creditors. Susannah Fielding played Portia as a blonde-wigged television celebrity who hosted her gameshow *Destiny* with canned laughter as a soundtrack as suitors chose their caskets. The show ended in Belmont, depicting a tormented Portia alone onstage, clutching her wig and wearing one high-heel, dancing to 'Are You Lonesome Tonight?'

TAMORA

TITUS ANDRONICUS

The evilest woman in Shakespeare?

SHOW ME A THOUSAND THAT HAVE DONE THEE WRONG, AND I'LL BE REVENGÈD ON THEM ALL.

ACT 5, SCENE 2

TAMORA

Titus Andronicus is thought to be one of Shakespeare's earliest plays and almost certainly his first tragedy. (Shakespeare didn't date his plays so we don't know exactly.) It gives the impression of the sixteenth-century equivalent of a student film made by a fan of horror who thinks they ought to make the most violent thing they can to be taken seriously. The events in the play are absolutely brutal and shocking, and you can't help but think, *Who exactly were you trying to appeal to here, Will?*

It's set in late-Roman times; the general Titus Andronicus has just come back from war and is the people's favourite to be elected emperor of Rome. Who knows what went on in this war (or what the people of Rome are hoping for from their leader)? We can only assume that everyone involved is heavily traumatised, such is the level of violence that follows. Shakespeare based the play on classical myth, rather than historical fact – thank God – so perhaps he intended it more as a gruesome allegory (an alle-gory?).

Titus brings home five prisoners from the war: Tamora, the queen of the Goths, who the Roman soldiers have been at war with, her three sons and Aaron, 'a Moor' (an historical term that initially described a particular group of Muslims from North Africa but was more commonly used in Europe to describe anyone with darker skin). Titus announces that he's going to kill Tamora's eldest son as part of the funeral rights for his 21 (*21!*) other sons who all died in the war. Tamora eloquently pleads for her son's life, arguing that he was fighting for his country, too, which the Romans are claiming is a noble and patriotic thing to do. 'Sweet mercy is nobility's true badge,' she says, totally misjudging her audience. (*It's a religious thing*, Titus responds, before the hacking-off of limbs commences.)

Furious and devastated, Tamora vows to take revenge. There are enough revenge killings in this play to make the most hardboiled gangster film look like a Disney movie.

Titus doesn't want to be emperor, he decides, so he supports Saturninus's application for the role against Saturninus's brother, Bassianus. He also hands over Tamora and her two living sons to Saturninus as a very weird gift. Saturninus and Bassianus both want to marry Lavinia, Titus's daughter. Titus says yes to Saturninus but barely a minute later Saturninus changes his mind and says he'll actually take Tamora – instantly elevating her from slave to empress. It's quite the turnaround. *Do you mind?* he says to Lavinia, not in the least caring about her answer.

Titus and Saturninus fall out. One of Titus's sons helps Bassianus carry off Lavinia and Titus kills him. Everything is in mad disarray and Tamora chooses this moment to start putting her revenge plan into action. *Let's all be friends*, says the new empress, playing the long game and fully intending to destroy them all.

Tamora is presumably reeling from the injustice of her son's ritual sacrifice, and it's true that both she and Aaron – who is Tamora's lover, it turns out – are subject to some vicious taunts about their heritage from Titus and his children. But it's also fair to say that, from here on in, Tamora is evil personified. She orders her sons to rape Lavinia, and they cut off her tongue and hands so she can't identify her assailants. They also murder Bassianus, and Aaron frames Quintus and Martius, two

WHEN YOU ARE TRYING TO BE THE PEACEMAKER TO TWO SQUABBLING FRIENDS:

... look graciously on him.
Lose not so noble a friend
on vain suppose,
Nor with sour looks afflict his
gentle heart.

WHEN YOUR MUM WON'T LET YOU BORROW THE CAR AGAIN:

Why hast thou slain thine only
daughter?

WHEN YOUR VISION FOR YOUR STYLISH PATIO GARDEN IS NOT WORKING OUT:

The trees, though summer, yet
forlorn and lean,
O'ercome with moss and baleful
mistletoe:
Here never shines the sun.

of Titus's surviving sons. They are to be executed, but even when Titus, his brother and the horribly mutilated Lavinia kneel to plead for their lives, Tamora is entirely without mercy. Aaron – who sees Tamora as his path to power – tricks Titus into cutting off his own hand, as he says his sons' lives will be spared in return. Obviously, they aren't. Their heads are returned along with the severed hand. When Tamora has Aaron's illegitimate baby, she wants it to be killed so as not to give away the paternity. Aaron instead substitutes a white baby and takes his own child back to the Goths for safekeeping (wise).

Like Titus and Saturninus, Tamora is entirely driven by revenge. She even dresses up as 'Revenge' personified to further mess with the understandably now-deranged Titus. Revenge is the big theme of the play and pretty much the only motivating plot device. And as the bodies pile up, everyone's insatiable desire for revenge only gets worse. Needless to say, many of the characters end up dead, with the exception of Titus's son Lucius, who goes on to unite with the Goths in order to violently take back Rome.

Tamora is clever, eloquent and a gifted master manipulator. She is also, it is safe to say, the most evil woman in Shakespeare's collective works. Goneril and Regan (see page 68) are deeply nasty, but even they would baulk at some of the things Tamora gets up to. She doesn't get away with it, of course – she is served up her sons' bodies baked into a pie before being stabbed to death by Titus (who is also killed). It's grim, horrible stuff. Really, all we can say about Tamora is that at least Shakespeare was all for equal gender opportunities when it came to evil.

RSC STAGE HISTORY

Sheila Hancock played Tamora in John Barton's 1981 production of *Titus Andronicus*, alongside Patrick Stewart as Titus. Hancock had recently finished performing as Mrs Lovett in *Sweeney Todd* and reprised her ghoulish pie-eating when she consumed her sons baked in a pie at the end of the play.

In the same season the duo also played opposite one another as Paulina (page 160) and Leontes in *The Winter's Tale*.

THE PRINCESS OF FRANCE

LOVE'S LABOUR'S LOST

Skilled diplomat trying to do her job

WE ARE WISE GIRLS TO MOCK OUR LOVERS SO.

ACT 5, SCENE 2

THE PRINCESS OF FRANCE

When the daughter of the King of France and her three accompanying ladies – Maria, Katherine and Rosaline – arrive in Navarre on a diplomatic mission, they are told to camp a mile away. For the princess, this is not good enough. She is a working professional, there to meet with the region's ruler, King Ferdinand, for some serious, high-level political business. 'Welcome to the court of Navarre,' says one of the king's trusted companions, Berowne, hopefully, when he meets the French delegation in the fields. The princess – who does not suffer fools – shuts him down: '. . . "welcome" I have not yet: the roof of this court is too high to be yours, and welcome to the wide fields too base to be mine.'

The reason for their non-admittance is that the somewhat pretentious Ferdinand has decided he wants to dedicate himself to study and make his court a hub of academic life. To avoid distractions, Ferdinand has devised a 'schedule' guaranteed to make him and his three companions – Berowne, Dumaine and Longaville – the most boring men ever. They will fast, sleep only a bit and avoid all contact with women. For three years. It's a bit like the sixteenth-century intellectual equivalent of daily workouts, protein shakes and ice baths. His friends are not overly keen but say they will go along with it, hoping he won't be able to stick to it.

You may have picked up that there are three women attending the princess, and the king has three friends, too. It's fairly obvious what's going to happen. Realising that her ladies-in-waiting have met Berowne, Dumaine and Longaville before, like any good politician, the princess asks for a briefing. But she is slightly taken aback by the praise they heap upon the Navarreans. 'God bless my ladies! Are they all in love . . . ?' she asks herself.

SHAKESPEARE'S STRONG WOMEN

WHEN THE FLATPACK ASSEMBLY INSTRUCTIONS ARE GETTING THE BETTER OF YOU:

Avaunt, perplexity!

WHEN YOUR FRIEND PROMISES THAT THEY'LL BE AT YOGA ON TUESDAY, HAVING MISSED THE LAST TWO:

Peace, peace, forbear.
Your oath once broke,
you force not to forswear.

WHAT TO DO WHEN A GIRLS' NIGHT OUT IS INTERRUPTED BY SOME UNWELCOME FLIRTING:

So shall we stay,
mocking intended game,
And they, well mocked, depart
away with shame.

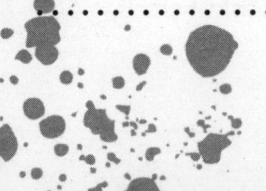

THE PRINCESS OF FRANCE

So, having taken an oath to eschew female company and not to fall in love, the men promptly do the opposite. They spend much of Acts 3 and 4 writing poems about the objects of their infatuations, overhearing each other declaim their poetry and sending letters that end up with the wrong people, creating the necessary comic confusion.

Love's Labour's Lost is one of Shakespeare's earliest comedies and the plot is less substantial than the threads and tangles and action scenes we find in plays like *A Midsummer Night's Dream* or *As You Like It*. Like Woody Allen or Aaron Sorkin, Shakespeare was mainly showcasing clever dialogue and witty comebacks when he wrote this play. It's now one of the least-performed works, mainly because the riffs on different sorts of poetry and drama that were around at the time and the satire of courtly behaviour are a bit lost on us. Some people see it as a kind of warm-up for *Much Ado About Nothing* – the verbal sparring between Rosaline and Berowne definitely has shades of the fun verbal jousting between Beatrice and Benedick (see page 26).

However, there are two other things that make this play particularly interesting. One is the princess herself. Apart from Portia's dabbling in the law, or the secondary characters who are maids or nurses, few Shakespearean women have anything we could call 'a job'. But here is the princess (who frustratingly doesn't have an actual name) out in the world with an important role, representing her father and her kingdom. She comes across as far cleverer than Ferdinand, who believes intellect is best served by staying at court and studying dead philosophers. She is authoritative, clear-sighted and pleasingly sarcastic. She holds no truck with flattery and empty compliments. 'Praise we may afford / To any lady that subdues a lord,' she says. Men may think they are in control, but a woman who really deserves a compliment is one who can take charge.

In the last scene of the play, the four women have received gifts and long, ridiculous poems from their admirers, which they compare and mock. Then, Boyet, an elderly lord who is the only male member of the princess's team, arrives to tell them that the king and his three friends – who by now know they are each in love with one of the French ladies – are going to visit them dressed, inexplicably, as Russians.

Well, in that case, says the princess, who is, of course, the kind of woman who can come up with a plan on the spot, let's mess with them. The four women put on masks and swap their gifts to confuse their suitors. It works and the men leave, to return shortly as themselves. The jokes and mockery continue until a messenger arrives with bad news: the princess's father is dead – which puts a bit of a downer on proceedings.

This is where the second fascinating element of *Love's Labour's Lost* comes in. Being a comedy, the play should end with at least one wedding. But Shakespeare denies us a traditional romantic ending. When the king proposes, the princess says he will have to wait a whole year while she mourns her father. In that time, he should go and shut himself away in a monastery. If he still wants her after 12 months, and his love is real and more than a load of grandiose compliments, then they'll get married. The other three women tell their suitors similar things.

Is this the princess trying to let the king down without causing a diplomatic incident? Or is she benching him in the hope that he'll grow up a bit and figure out what love really means? 'Our wooing doth not end like an old play,' observes Berowne. *We only have to wait a year*, says the king. 'That's too long for a play,' Berowne replies, meta-ly.

The realities of love and forming a meaningful partnership with someone aren't accurately reflected in romcoms, Shakespeare may be saying here. Will the princess really marry the king in a year? Whatever her plan is, it's sure to be a good one. This astute and perceptive diplomat, with her take-no-prisoners wit, always seems to know exactly what she's doing.

RSC STAGE HISTORY

In 2024, director Emily Burns and designer Joanna Scotcher set the production on a tech bro's luxury island, complete with spa and golf course, with the men forfeiting their phones for study. Melanie-Joyce Bermudez played a Pacific Island princess who opened and closed the show speaking and singing in her native language.

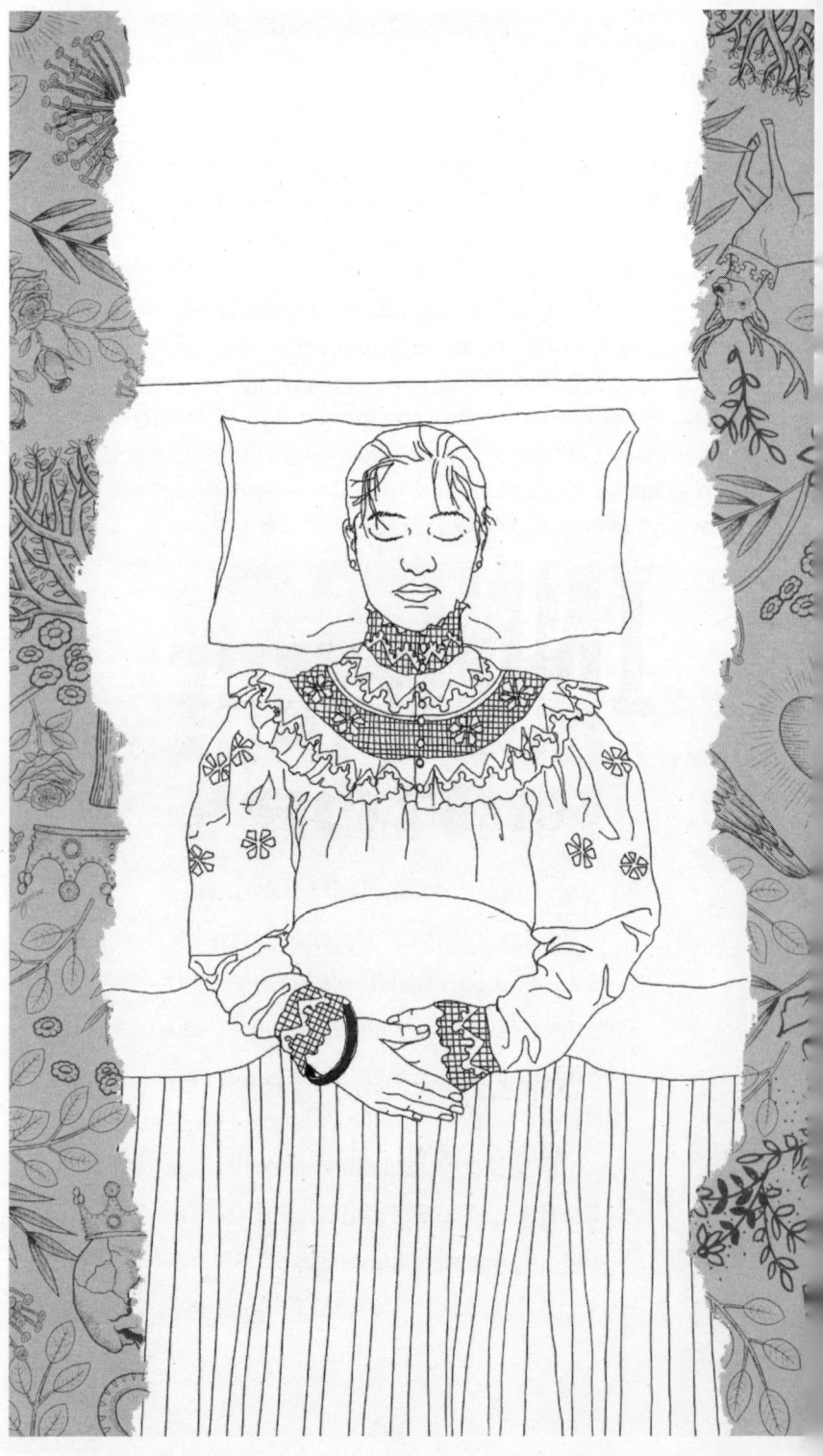

INNOGEN

CYMBELINE

Steadfast heroine holds her nerve

I SEE A MAN'S LIFE IS A TEDIOUS ONE.

ACT 3, SCENE 6

INNOGEN

One of Shakespeare's later plays, *Cymbeline* contains quite a lot of rather familiar elements that, if we were Shakespeare's publicist, we might call 'signature tropes' rather than 'using the same ideas again'. We have: a wronged daughter, someone claiming a woman is unfaithful for no good reason, a woman who runs away from the court and pretends to be a man and long-lost children. But we also get a great female main character, who is at the emotional heart of the play *and* gets more lines than anyone else. Yippee!

The play is still pretty dark, though. Cymbeline is the King of Britain. Since the abduction of his sons when they were young, his daughter, Innogen, is his only heir. He wants her to marry her stepbrother, Cloten, the son of his second wife, who enjoys manipulating people and killing small animals with poison. But she has in fact married Posthumus, a man with a name that it's hard to take seriously, given to him because his dad died before he was born.

> *That I, which know my heart, do here pronounce By th' very truth of it, I care not for you.*
> **ACT 2, SCENE 3**

One of Innogen's defining characteristics is that she is very loyal – particularly to Posthumus, though we are given many reasons to question if he deserves it. And he has to spend most of the play learning to deserve it. When he is banished from court by Innogen's angry dad, the couple exchange tokens

WHEN SOMEONE IS CONSTANTLY
NEGGING YOU:

*O dissembling courtesy!
How fine this tyrant
Can tickle where she wounds!*

WHEN YOU REALLY NEED A
COLLEAGUE TO ACTION YOUR EMAIL:

*Those things I bid you do,
get them dispatched.*

WHEN YOU'RE WONDERING IF THE GUY
YOU MATCHED WITH HAS GOOD CHAT AS
WELL AS GOOD LOOKS:

*Is he disposed to mirth?
I hope he is.*

INNOGEN

of their enduring love. She hands him a ring that belonged to her mum, giving him permission to offer it to his next wife when she is dead. He gives her a bracelet, saying, rather ominously, that 'It is a manacle of love. I'll place it / Upon this fairest prisoner.'

We first see Cloten after he's had a fight with Posthumus, which he says he wishes hadn't been broken up, as he definitely would have battered him (other reports differ). One of the men listening to this posturing story responds in an aside, 'So would I, till you had measured how long a fool you were upon the ground.' Innogen calls him a 'puttock' – an insult meaning a rubbish bird of prey known for being greedy and scavenging. It seems everyone thinks he's an idiot – though he's going to show that he's a dangerous idiot.

Posthumus is also a bit of an idiot. He reaches Rome, where he lets nasty, slimy Iachimo wind him up. *I bet you a load of money against that ring that I could sleep with this wife of yours that you keep going on about*, he goads. *Fine*, says Posthumus. When Iachimo reaches the British court and tries his luck with Innogen she obviously roundly rejects him. He lies that Posthumus is gallivanting around Rome sleeping with sex workers, but, loyal as she is, she won't believe him. He creepily sneaks into her bedroom while she's asleep, gets a look at a mole on her breast

> *To lapse in fullness*
> *Is sorer than to lie for*
> *need, and falsehood*
> *Is worse in kings than*
> *beggars.*
>
> **ACT 3, SCENE 6**

and steals the bracelet, which he uses to convince Posthumus that he has won the bet. Posthumus – showing a lot less faith in Innogen than she has in him, and much less than she deserves – goes off on one about how all women are horrible and not to be trusted. He writes to Innogen to tell her to meet him in Milford Haven (of all places). Not only does he stand her up, but he instructs his servant Pisanio to kill her.

> *There cannot be a pinch in death More sharp than this is.*
>
> ACT 1, SCENE 1

Even when Pisanio tells Innogen what Posthumus has asked him to do, she stays loyal to him, despite being devastated. Pisanio's solution to the problem is for Innogen to dress as a boy and he will tell Posthumus she is dead. Why not, right? While pretending to be 'Fidele' – a pun on 'fidelity', of course – she meets two young men, who later turn out to be the brothers that were abducted as children. This is lucky, as Cloten is on her trail and plans to rape her in revenge for her rejection of him, but one of her brothers ends up beheading him after they get into a fight. However, Cloten is wearing clothes belonging to Posthumus (don't ask), so Innogen thinks the headless body is that of her love.

It's been observed by critics that in Shakespeare's comedies women often show men how to behave better; they learn the error of their ways, and the bravery and loyalty of the female characters lead to them getting second chances. In tragedies,

INNOGEN

however, men's jealousy, hubris, poor decision-making and emotional volatility usually lead to everyone dying. Cymbeline is officially classified as a tragedy, though no one quite knows why, as it actually follows the structure of a comedy. Posthumus is later wracked with guilt for ordering the murder of Innogen – his solution is to try to get himself killed in a war between Britain and Rome. Fortunately, Innogen, of course, sorts it all out.

> *O, Men's vows are women's traitors. All good seeming, By thy revolt, O husband, shall be thought Put on for villainy; not born where't grows, But worn a bait for ladies.*
>
> **ACT 3, SCENE 4**

For reasons that are too longwinded to go into, forthright Innogen – still pretending to be Fidele – is granted the opportunity to cross-examine Iachimo after he is captured alongside Posthumus in the war. Iachimo confesses to his terrible behaviour, and Posthumus understands what happened and expresses how sorry he is. And he doesn't kill Iachimo when he gets the chance, which represents some growth of sorts.

The discovery of Innogen's true identity leads to the revelation of her brothers' identity, and she generously forgives her father for trying to force her to marry the horrendous Cloten. Her dad seems to have mellowed, too, no doubt helped by the death of his villainous second wife, who has conveniently revealed her many misdemeanours on her deathbed.

So Posthumus and Innogen are reunited. Let's hope that Posthumus continues to learn from Innogen's bravery and faithfulness. The couple presumably won't rule Britain together now that Innogen's brothers have turned up, but those guys grew up on a hill in Wales and need to get up to speed on court politics. So, let's assume they will recognise Innogen's abilities and ensure she gets a powerful position that makes the most of her integrity and skill.

RSC STAGE HISTORY

Emma Fielding played Innogen opposite Daniel Evans as Posthumus in Dominic Cooke's 2003 production. Her performance as Innogen was praised for being 'tough' and 'gritty' rather than an idealised image of female purity. Rae Smith's designs juxtaposed the Ancient Britons in feathers and furs with the Italians in chic white suits and sunglasses. Twenty years later, Daniel Evans went on to become co-artistic director of the RSC in 2023, and Emma Fielding became an associate artist for the RSC, performing in numerous productions.

MARGARET OF ANJOU

HENRY VI, PART 1;
HENRY VI, PART 2;
HENRY VI, PART 3
AND RICHARD III

Do not mess with Margaret

O, TIGER'S HEART WRAPT IN A WOMAN'S HIDE!

DUKE OF YORK, HENRY VI, PART 3, ACT 1, SCENE 4

MARGARET OF ANJOU

Whatever you think of Margaret of Anjou, you can't deny that she gets a brilliant character arc through her appearances in the first four outings of Shakespeare's Wars of the Roses franchise. She was a real person, of course, but Shakespeare didn't let facts get in the way. In Margaret, he created a uniquely powerful and ruthless female leader.

When we first meet her, at the end of *Henry VI, Part 1*, Margaret has been taken prisoner by the Duke of Suffolk. He is a battle-hardened English aristocrat, probably in his forties. She is the daughter of the impoverished Reignier, Duke of Anjou, and a teenager. She is scared but brave, showing an interesting mix of naivety and wisdom. She is obviously worried about what this enemy soldier is planning for her. 'What ransom must I pay?' she asks with trepidation, confused by Suffolk's slightly weird behaviour.

He is acting oddly because he has fallen instantly for the 'princely majesty' of her beauty. 'She is a woman, therefore to be won,' he thinks, but he also refers to her as 'a sweet child', which is a bit grim. He remembers he is already married and decides to make the young and impressionable King Henry marry her instead. And so enters the new Queen of England, who is set to become one of Shakespeare's most influential and terrifying female characters.

The first speech in *Henry VI, Part 2* is about Margaret, which tells us that she is going to be important. I married her for you, says Suffolk when presenting her to Henry, who doesn't seem to think he has overstepped any boundaries at all. Suffolk's plan is to control the king through Margaret, with the added bonus of keeping the object of his creepy crush close to him.

WHEN THE FRONT GARDEN HAS
TURNED INTO A JUNGLE:

*Now 'tis the spring,
and weeds are shallow-rooted:
Suffer them now,
and they'll o'ergrow the garden
And choke the herbs for
want of husbandry.*

WHEN YOU'RE VERY HAPPY WITH YOUR
CHOICE OF MEME ON THE GROUP CHAT:

Herein I judge mine own wit good.

WHEN YOU CAN SEE YOUR FRIEND'S NEW BEAU
IS A WRONG 'UN BUT THEY WON'T LISTEN:

*What, dost thou scorn me
for my gentle counsel?
And soothe the devil that
I warn thee from?
O, but remember this another day,
When he shall split thy very
heart with sorrow.*

However, he has underestimated Margaret and so has everyone else.

Far more switched on than her dozy young husband, Margaret quickly learns the ways of the power-hungry, scheming men around her at court. On the one hand, she is doing Suffolk's bidding in this play, but his aims suit her, too, and by working with him to get rid of his rival, the Duke of Gloucester, she is taking more power for herself.

It's not made explicit whether they are sleeping together, but Margaret does seem to be genuinely in love with Suffolk. After Suffolk's death, Henry says to her, 'I fear me, love, if that I had been dead, / Thou wouldst not have mourned so much for me.' And she is devastated when he dies. Yes, it's an age-inappropriate relationship that started with a huge power imbalance, but Margaret has come a long way from the captured French girl she was at the end of the previous play. We can't always tell who is pulling whose strings.

At the beginning of the third instalment, Henry's reign is under immediate threat from the Duke of York. Henry agrees to make York his heir, disinheriting his own son, Prince Edward. Margaret is absolutely not standing for that. Her ineffectual husband flaps about uselessly while Margaret raises an army. So, she's now a mother – though when she had time to give birth is anyone's guess, as Shakespeare doesn't really get into that; Edward just appears as a child already able to talk. And she is also a warrior queen, ruthlessly directing battles.

A lot of people seem openly terrified of her now, and with good reason – she has dialled it all the way up to 11. When the Duke of York is captured, she torments him by putting a paper crown on his head and gives him a handkerchief dipped in the blood of his recently murdered son. 'And if thine eyes can water for his death, / I give thee this to dry thy cheeks withal,' she tells him, giving Hannibal Lecter vibes.

By the end of the play, both Henry and Prince Edward are dead. Despite delivering a rousing speech to her troops, the Battle of Tewkesbury is lost. Margaret gets her cosmic comeuppance for doing exactly what all the men around her have been doing all the way through – scheming for power. She is grief-stricken at the loss of her son and asks to be killed by her captors, too, but they refuse. Though Richard (as in the future Richard III) disagrees with this decision: 'Why should she live to fill the world with words?' he asks, inadvertently flagging her brilliant way with language.

The real Margaret of Anjou died in exile in France, but Shakespeare brings her back to England in *Richard III*. Here she is more rage-filled spectre than woman, haunting the court of the murderers of her husband and son, dependent on their charity. She doesn't have an awful lot to do, but serves as a reminder of the violence done to get power and of the high cost of ambition. She curses them – *a lot*; there's nothing they can do to make her stop or leave – and tells them of the evil that's in their midst.

Margaret is the only character who appears in all four of these plays (the 'first tetralogy', academics call them). She is such a fascinating character and a powerful presence that it's not surprising Shakespeare couldn't leave her out. You can almost imagine Margaret herself insisting on it as he was writing. She is eloquent in her malevolence, utterly committed, and everything that her ill-equipped husband is not. Lady

Macbeth would have loved to have had the influence that Margaret wielded, and Cleopatra probably would have been scared of her. The Duke of York famously calls her the 'she-wolf of France', which, if you ignore the context, sounds rather aspirational.

RSC STAGE HISTORY

Peggy Ashcroft played Margaret of Anjou in John Barton's famous *Wars of the Roses* plays in 1963. In a monumental performance, she aged from a young girl to a ferocious, vengeful crone through the histories cycle. Ashcroft adopted a French 'R' sound to emphasise the character's alien status in the English court. She was so intrinsic to the RSC's history that one of its most famous rehearsal spaces, the wooden-beamed Ashcroft Room above the Swan Theatre, is named after her.

MIRANDA

THE TEMPEST

*Sweet-natured girl
has had a weird childhood*

HOW BEAUTEOUS MANKIND IS! O BRAVE NEW WORLD, THAT HAS SUCH PEOPLE IN'T!

ACT 5, SCENE 1

MIRANDA

> *Before considering the strange nature of Miranda's childhood we should acknowledge that* The Tempest *is a problematic text. Post-colonial readings of the play show that Caliban has been exploited by Prospero through his occupation of his island. Contemporary productions will often draw out this unfair treatment of Caliban and want the audience to question and feel unsettled by it.*

Since she was three years old, Miranda has grown up on an island with only her dad (a bossy magician prone to repeating himself) and his slaves – indigenous islander Caliban and magical Ariel – for company. She is compassionate and full of wonder, but, now aged fifteen, she is completely innocent, unaware of anything outside of her tiny world. And she is about to fall in love with the first boy she sees.

As her dad, Prospero, has been her sole companion, parent and teacher, he is a big influence on her. He's an authoritarian presence (his colonisation of the island and its inhabitants make for uncomfortable viewing) and Miranda is respectfully obedient to his wishes – though she does push back occasionally, showing that she has a mind of her own and there is an independent spirit lurking there somewhere, even if she hasn't had the chance to figure out who she is yet.

The Tempest opens with – unsurprisingly – a massive storm. Miranda and Prospero watch a ship floundering in the waves, with empathetic Miranda

> *I would not wish*
> *Any companion in*
> *the world but you:*
> *Nor can imagination*
> *form a shape*
> *Besides yourself to*
> *like of.*
>
> **ACT 3, SCENE 1**

panicking about the poor passengers and crew. *Don't worry*, says Prospero self-importantly, *I have magicked up the whole thing and I promise that no one is going to get hurt.*

He then proceeds to tell Miranda her origin story, which he has kept from her until now. Prospero was in fact the Duke of Milan, but while he wasn't paying attention, his conniving brother, Antonio, usurped him, stuck Prospero and the infant Miranda in a leaky boat and set them adrift on the sea. Luckily, a nice man called Gonzalo had put some food and water in the boat, so they didn't die and instead washed up on the island. *I must have been such a burden to you, being so little*, says Miranda. *No, you were what kept me going*, says Prospero. He is a controlling, interfering father, but there is real love here.

It recently came to Prospero's attention, however, that his brother was on a boat that was going to sail past the island, along with the King of Naples, Alonso (who was also complicit in the plot against him) and the king's son, Ferdinand. So, with the help of Ariel, his sprite-like assistant, Prospero conjured the storm to wreck them on the island and get his dukedom back.

According to his plan, the shipwrecked men have been separated and dotted around the island, not knowing whether the others survived. Miranda and Prospero first encounter Ferdinand, who Miranda immediately falls in love with. He feels the same and Prospero is delighted, as it's a great match and all in line with his scheme. However, he pretends not to be pleased – maybe because opposing the match is useful for the play's plot and pretty much always the job of a Shakespearean dad. He proceeds to make Ferdinand's life difficult, accusing him of being a spy and making him do hard labour. (Forcing other people to do his bidding is very much Prospero's 'thing'.) Miranda tries to stand up for Ferdinand while making excuses for Prospero's behaviour: 'My father's of a better nature, sir, / Than he appears by speech.'

Ferdinand does seem like a very sweet boy who is genuinely enthralled by Miranda. When she gamely offers to help him carry the logs Prospero has instructed him to move, she tells Ferdinand her name, even though it seems her dad has forbidden this. Ferdinand tells her, slightly annoyingly, that he's liked 'several women' before but they all had something wrong with them, while Miranda is 'created / Of every creature's best'. Despite not knowing any other men than her father, she tells Ferdinand, 'I would not wish / Any companion in the world but you.' In her unaffected, straight-talking way, she asks him if he loves her, and when he says he does, she asks him if he'll be her husband. Prospero is secretly watching all of this, a little creepily.

In some ways, *The Tempest* is like the anti-*Hamlet*. Rather than one brother killing another, Prospero exposes Antonio's treachery, reclaims his power and forgives his brother, even though Antonio doesn't seem at all sorry. Miranda is a little like Ophelia (see page 34) in her sweetness and innocence, and in the way those characteristics work as a plot device. And similarly, she is pushed around by a controlling dad, who spies on her interactions with a man she likes. But rather than being trapped in a 'rotten' court, she has grown up on a beautiful island – nature often being a force for good in Shakespeare's plays, where characters have more freedom to do and be what they want.

Miranda is charming and often forthright, presumably because she hasn't grown up adhering to the social conventions of a 'courtly' woman. Early in the play, Prospero mentions that Caliban once tried to rape her. Caliban confirms this and Miranda calls out what she sees as his inherent evil in lines that seem so vitriolic and out of character that some academics think they must have been intended for Prospero and misattributed: 'Abhorrèd slave, / Which any print of goodness wilt not take, / Being capable of all ill.' While Caliban shows no remorse for his actions to Miranda, post-colonial readings of the play remind us that Caliban has been exploited and abused by Prospero (and, by proxy, Miranda, too) through occupation of his island, which has become his prison.

> *Good wombs have borne bad sons.*
>
> **ACT 1, SCENE 2**

The play ends with all of Prospero's magical manipulations working out so that everyone is reconciled and reunited. They get ready to go back to Naples, where Miranda and Ferdinand will officially be married, bringing together the two families. We can't help but wonder how Miranda will get on at the Neapolitan court, having no concept of any kind of society. Will it be a *Mean Girls* scenario? Like Lindsay Lohan's character, Cady, will she be picked on by the ladies at court? Or will she meet a load of handsome courtiers and realise that Ferdinand is not actually all that? Alternatively, she does say that she has never seen another woman, so maybe the gorgeous Italian women will be more appealing? Hopefully, her natural charm will see her through, and getting out from under the shadow of her dad will give her the opportunity to find out more about herself, as she discovers the world beyond her childhood home.

WHEN SOME DETAILS OF LAST
NIGHT'S PARTY ARE HAZY:

'Tis far off
And rather like a dream
than an assurance
That my remembrance warrants.

WHEN YOU GET EMOTIONAL OVER
A LOVELY BIRTHDAY GIFT:

I am a fool
To weep at what I am glad of.

WARNING YOUR COLLEAGUE THAT YOUR
BOSS IS IN A TERRIBLE MOOD:

Never till this day
Saw I him touched with anger,
so distempered.

RSC STAGE HISTORY

In 2006 Mariah Gale played an earnest Miranda to her dominating father, Prospero, played by Patrick Stewart. Rupert Goold's production was set on an Arctic wilderness island with costumes inspired by traditional Inuit designs. Gale went on to play many of Shakespeare's strong women at the RSC, including Juliet (see page 92), the Princess of France (see page 188), Queen Margaret (see page 206) and Ophelia (see page 34).

CRESSIDA

TROILUS AND CRESSIDA

Trojan war makes dating difficult

BOLDNESS COMES TO ME NOW, AND BRINGS ME HEART.

ACT 3, SCENE 2

CRESSIDA

Here we are at the famous Trojan war, which of course started because Paris stole the Greek king's beautiful wife, Helen. It's been dragging on for ages and the combatants on each side are getting ratty with each other. It's got the vibe of a lads' holiday that's gone on way too long and no one can remember why they even wanted to go to Ibiza in the first place.

This is the backdrop to a love story between two young Trojans, Troilus and Cressida – except the play is more concerned with the fighting and falling-out, so it's not really a backdrop. And the love story isn't really much of one. Romeo and Juliet (see page 92) or Antony and Cleopatra (see page 58) they ain't. In fact, their relationship barely gets off the ground.

Cressida's uncle, pervy Pandarus, is keen that Cressida get with Troilus. He praises him to the heavens (to the point where we almost wonder if *he* would like to get with Troilus – 'I could live and die i' th' eyes of Troilus'). It's all very over the top and Cressida banters with him wittily, undermining or wilfully misunderstanding the compliments. Pandarus complains that Cressida is hard to read and gives nothing away. *Of course not*, she says. *I have to be on my guard. Particularly against gossip.*

This feels like a sensible strategy. Not least because Cressida's father, Calchas, has defected to the Greek side, which presumably makes her position in the Trojan court a little awkward. But Cressida *does* like Troilus, as she tells us in soliloquy. It's just that she knows that men tend to want what they can't have – they 'prize the thing ungained more than it is'. So she wants to enjoy his wooing of her and also not make it too easy for him.

This sounds sensible, too. Cressida, it seems, is a savvy lady.

To be honest, though, Troilus seems like a bit of a wet lettuce, and we wonder if he is worthy of her anyway. We know he's only twenty-two, that he can't grow a beard, and Pandarus tells us he's the soft and sentimental type. All of which are fine, of course, but he doesn't sound right for whip-smart Cressida.

Slap bang in the middle of the play, pervy Pandy gets the couple together in an orchard. 'I am giddy; expectation whirls me round,' says Troilus, sounding like a high-schooler with a crush, as he anticipates their meeting. After more meddling from her uncle, who really could just leave them to it, Cressida admits to Troilus that she does like him. 'Prince Troilus, I have loved you night and day / For many weary months,' she says poetically. *Why were you playing hard to get, then?* Troilus asks prosaically. *Because I'm a woman and it's your job to woo me!* she tells him.

Troilus vows to be remembered as the truest Troilus that ever there was, and Cressida says that if she ever cheats on him, let people use the expression 'as false as Cressid' about anyone who lies. Which is really tempting fate – something that people in classical stories know you should never do. Off they go to consummate their love in a bedroom sourced for them by Pandarus, who would like history to remember him as someone who helped young couples get it on. Yuck.

> *They say all lovers swear more performance than they are able.*
> **ACT 3, SCENE 2**

WHEN YOU NEED TO REMEMBER TO ENJOY THE PROCESS, NOT JUST THE OUTCOME:

Things won are done, joy's soul lies in the doing.

WHEN YOU DECIDE TO FOLLOW YOUR FRIEND'S OUT-THERE ADVICE:

What folly I commit, I dedicate to you.

WHEN YOU WENT TO BED WAAAY TOO LATE:

Night hath been too brief.

But in the morning there is bad news. Cressida's dad has negotiated her exchange for a Trojan prisoner, Antenor (the TV signal is bad without him), so she is going to have to leave Troy and join the Greek camp. Cressida would much rather no one knew that she slept with Troilus, but Aeneas barges into her chambers looking for him, so presumably everyone knows there is something going on between them.

> *Sweet, bid me hold my tongue, For in this rapture I shall surely speak The thing I shall repent.*
>
> **ACT 3, SCENE 2**

Cressida is devastated to have to leave Troilus – 'The grief is fine, full, perfect, that I taste' – and they exchange love tokens. He admits he is worried she will cheat on him with the 'merry Greeks', who are well known for their charming ways. *What?!* says Cressida. *Absolutely not.*

However, no sooner does she reach the Greek camp than she starts to flirt. Achilles, Agamemnon and Nestor all kiss her in welcome, and she banters coquettishly with Menelaus and Ulysses – the latter of whom doesn't seem to have a particularly high opinion of her. She is then taken off by Diomedes.

Cressida is in a dangerous situation – she has very little protection if any of the Greeks decide to rape her. Is she fawning to try to get their affection and protection? She's very aware that she is a woman stuck in the middle of a war that's been dragging on for years, being used as a bargaining chip. Diomedes makes her promise that she will have sex with him, though he seems to be losing patience with her and keeps threatening to storm out, as he says she is making a fool of him. She is reluctant but keeps calling him back. He demands a token from her, so she gives the gift that Troilus gave her, then immediately regrets it and tries to take it back. Unfortunately, Troilus, who has snuck into the Greek camp, witnesses the whole thing. Including her whispering in Diomedes' ear (which is annoying, as we want to know what she said). Later, she sends him a letter that he reads and tears up. We don't know what's in that either, but it's clear that Troilus and Cressida are definitely over.

> *Prithee, do not hold me*
> *to mine oath:*
> *Bid me do anything*
> *but that.*
>
> **ACT 5, SCENE 2**

Shakespeare based the war bits of the play on *The Iliad*, the famous epic poem that the Elizabethans enjoyed, and so would have been familiar to his audience. However, Troilus and Cressida are a bolt-on, borrowed from Chaucer, who in turn borrowed them from other medieval sources. Shakespeare seems to be satirising the apparent heroism and nobility of war with the squabbling, posturing Greeks and Trojans, and the idea of romantic, courtly love through Troilus and Cressida.

Though so many of the men Shakespeare created are obsessed to varying degrees with the chastity and fidelity of the women in their lives, almost none are actually unfaithful (as we assume Cressida is, although Shakespeare doesn't spell it out). So it would have been great to know more of Cressida's motivation. She seems so playful and sharp at the beginning; it would be fun if she had just decided that Troilus wasn't a great lover and Diomedes was much better looking. However, it feels like Emilia from *Othello* (see page 264), who seems to have thought more about why women are unfaithful than anyone else, would sympathise with her predicament. We learn that war is as dangerous for women as it is for men, just in a different way.

> *Well, well, 'tis done, 'tis past. And yet it is not: I will not keep my word.*
>
> **ACT 5, SCENE 2**

RSC STAGE HISTORY

Sam Mendes's 1996 modern production in the Swan Theatre mixed 'clean-limbed' Trojans with 'grungy Greeks' and starred Ralph Fiennes as Troilus opposite Amanda Root as Cressida. Root's Cressida was played more as a 'tragic victim than flirtatious main character', while Fiennes's self-absorbed Troilus seemed to be 'more in love with voice music than the girl'.

ISABELLA

MEASURE FOR MEASURE

Actually do get thee to a nunnery

O, IT IS EXCELLENT TO HAVE A GIANT'S STRENGTH, BUT IT IS TYRANNOUS TO USE IT LIKE A GIANT.

ACT 2, SCENE 2

ISABELLA

Isabella is a smart, articulate young woman who wants to become a nun. As the play progresses, we see why she'd prefer to live in a convent for the rest of her life. *The Sound of Music* this is not.

Isabella receives word that her brother has been imprisoned and sentenced to death, and he wants her to go and plead for his life. His 'crime' is that his fiancée, Juliet, is pregnant. They were going to get married, Claudio says, they were just waiting to get some money. Juliet shows up briefly to tell us that she loves Claudio and it was all consensual, but in the new world order of Vienna, this is not good enough.

Isabella doesn't think she has any power to help, but, even though her beliefs mean that she doesn't approve of her brother's behaviour, off she goes to see the new man in charge, Angelo. Lord Angelo has been tasked with a clean-up operation in Vienna – no more brothels and people doing whatever they like. We're told that his 'blood / Is very snow-broth' – he is immune to the usual human temptations of the body.

Angelo has been given the job by Duke Vincentio, the man who usually runs Vienna. He claims he has got to go on a work trip to Poland, but really he is going to dress as a friar and hang around to see 'if power change purpose' – i.e., if Angelo remains so moral and passionless when he is in charge. The real friar from whom he borrows his disguise points out that the duke could have sorted out the situation in Vienna himself, but the duke makes the excuse that it would be 'tyranny' to suddenly start punishing people for what he has previously allowed them to do. Which sounds a lot like he doesn't want to act the bad cop. Someone else can do it instead.

At first, Isabella is a bit tongue-tied in front of Angelo, but she finds her voice and eloquently argues that mercy is more important than the letter of the law; it's not for humans to judge like God when they are all fallible and prone to making mistakes. As a young woman of little status, to lecture a powerful man by telling him to examine his own guilt before he judges others seems a risky business: 'Go to your bosom, / Knock there, and ask your heart what it doth know / That's like my brother's fault.' That said, it seems to work, as a flustered Angelo asks her to come back tomorrow.

However, Angelo then says he will only spare her brother's life if Isabella sleeps with him – an outrageous condition that exposes him as a dirty hypocrite. Her virtue turns him on, basically. She threatens to tell everyone and he says – in words that sadly echo down the centuries – that no one will believe her because he is a powerful man with a certain reputation and she is just a woman. And what's more, if she doesn't agree, not only will the execution of her brother go ahead, but he'll be tortured, too.

Isabella then has the horrible task of telling her brother that she can't give up her honour for his life; she believes she will be damned for all eternity if she commits this sin. At first Claudio agrees, but – scared and having a bit of an existential crisis – he then changes his tune: 'What sin you

> *Go to your bosom,*
> *Knock there, and ask*
> *your heart what it*
> *doth know.*
>
> **ACT 2, SCENE 2**

do to save a brother's life, / Nature dispenses with the deed so far / That it becomes a virtue.' Isabella is devastated. She's already been put in a horrific position by Angelo and now her brother is making it worse.

The eavesdropping duke in his friar costume now pops up to intervene. He has a plan! Is it to reveal himself as the duke, march over to Angelo and give him what for, as is totally within his power? No! He tells them that Angelo was supposed to have married a woman called Mariana but reneged on his promise at the last minute because her dowry was lost at sea. *She'd probably pretend to be you and sleep with Angelo instead*, he suggests. 'The hand that hath made you fair hath made you good,' he says to Isabella, somewhat creepily, when dressed as a man of God. It's getting more and more messed up by the minute.

How do we feel about Isabella agreeing to this plan? The idea is that Angelo will then have to marry Mariana, but surely this isn't a nailed-on certainty? There's a sense that Mariana is being thrown under a bus here. She agrees offstage, but we trust that Isabella has told her the exact truth of the situation and Mariana still chooses to take her chances with the vile Angelo.

Despite Isabella having told Angelo she will sleep with him, he orders her brother's execution anyway,

> *Truth is truth*
> *To th'end of*
> *reck'ning.*
>
> **ACT 5, SCENE 1**

WHEN YOU REALLY CAN'T SEEM TO MAKE A DECISION:

*I am
At war 'twixt will and will not.*

WHEN YOU'RE TRYING TO DECIDE WHETHER TO LEAVE A BAD REVIEW OF SOME TERRIBLE SERVICE:

*To whom should I complain?
Did I tell this,
Who would believe me?*

HOW TO MAKE AN ENTRANCE AT A DINNER PARTY THAT SHAKESPEARE WOULD APPROVE OF:

What, ho! Peace here, grace and good company

so the duke comes up with yet another plan, this time using the severed head of a recently deceased prisoner to convince Angelo that his orders have been carried out. Angelo goes ahead and has sex with the woman he

> *I do think that you might pardon him, And neither heaven nor man grieve at the mercy.*
>
> **ACT 2, SCENE 2**

thinks is Isabella, like the absolute bastard he is, while the duke-pretending-to-be-a-friar lets Isabella think her brother is dead – like the absolute bastard he also is.

The duke returns as himself and Isabella makes an impassioned and brave speech, saying – in front of everyone – that, to her shame, she did have sex with Angelo and he killed her brother anyway. Mariana reveals her part in the plot and her prior betrothal to Angelo. The duke lets this go on for ages before he admits that he was the meddling friar. He sentences Angelo to marry Mariana and then to be executed for the death of Claudio. Mariana convinces Isabella to plead for Angelo – which she does. The duke's final *ta-da!* is to produce a living Claudio. Incredibly pleased with himself, he then asks Isabella to marry him. Dude, after all you have put her through? And she wants to be *a nun*!! Were you not listening?

Isabella says nothing. She gets no more lines. There has been no suggestion that she was developing feelings for the duke-dressed-as-a-friar. In fact, she trusted him as a man of God, but he turned out to be a fake, sneaking around, hearing confessions, getting into everyone's business. Surely, she is going to run back to the convent as fast as she can? Ultimately, we can't be sure of her fate – whether she goes to a nunnery or a church to be married; Shakespeare leaves this 'problem play' open to interpretation.

It *is* a weird play, but also a fascinating one. Isabella follows her own path, clinging to her virtue and faith, while all the men around her behave appallingly, trying to convince her to do the opposite of what she knows to be right. Is the duke's love meant to be a reward? The play asks a load of questions – about power, justice, belief; when is a sin a sin? – and leaves us to think about the answers. Isabella's strength and steadfast belief in what is right are the only certainties here.

RSC STAGE HISTORY

Juliet Stevenson played an Isabella in 1983 that was full of passion, intelligence and courage, as well as principle. She said of the role, 'The fascination for me was taking away the judgements about her – like... Isabella is frigid because she won't sleep with Angelo – let's look at why these women are making these choices. What power do they have? What do they not have?' Her luminous performance earned her an Olivier Award nomination in 1984.

JULIA AND SILVIA

THE TWO GENTLEMEN OF VERONA

Two ladies who deserve better

IT IS THE LESSER BLOT, MODESTY FINDS, WOMEN TO CHANGE THEIR SHAPES THAN MEN THEIR MINDS.

JULIA
ACT 5, SCENE 4

THOU SUBTLE, PERJURED, FALSE, DISLOYAL MAN: THINK'ST THOU I AM SO SHALLOW, SO CONCEITLESS, TO BE SEDUCED BY THY FLATTERY, THAT HAST DECEIVED SO MANY WITH THY VOWS?

SILVIA
ACT 4, SCENE 2

JULIA AND SILVIA

The Two Gentlemen of Verona is a story about how two perfectly nice women get stuck in the middle of a co-dependent bromance between two guys called Proteus and Valentine. Spoiler alert: one in particular is most definitely *not* a gentleman.

Over the course of the play, Julia proves herself to be brave, steadfast, independent and more than capable of carrying out a plan once she has committed to it. But when we first meet her in Act 1, Scene 2, she seems a bit silly and flaky. She is asking her maid Lucetta to go through a list of her suitors and say what she thinks of them. When Proteus's name comes up, Julia jumps on it, while pretending she's not bothered. Lucetta produces a letter that she thinks is from him and Julia claims to be angry that Lucetta accepted it on her behalf. Then she decides she does want to read it. Then she tears it up so she can't. Then, when she's alone, she tries to piece it back together again and we see that she does really like him.

Before this, however, in the very first scene, we witness a heartfelt moment between the couple whose relationship is really at the heart of the play. Valentine's dad thinks it would be good for him to travel, so he's off to Milan on a sort of gap year. He'd like his best friend, Proteus, to come with him, but Proteus is going to stay behind because he is in love with Julia. Valentine is possibly a bit jealous. *Love is stupid*, he says, *and it's ruling your life*: 'Love is your master, for he masters you.' They promise to write to each other and off Valentine goes.

Proteus's dad has had enough of him dossing about at home and decides he needs to go and make something of himself, so he sends Proteus off to join

WHEN YOU LOVE YOUR NEW NOISE-CANCELLING HEADPHONES:

This babble shall not henceforth trouble me.

WHEN YOUR MIND'S WHIRRING AND YOU CAN'T GET TO SLEEP:

It hath been the longest night That e'er I watched, and the most heaviest.

SARCASTICALLY, WHEN YOU ARE GETTING A BIT TIRED OF THE PUB BANTS:

A fine volley of words, gentlemen, and quickly shot off.

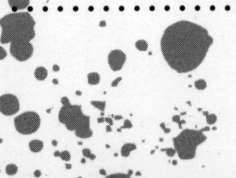

JULIA AND SILVIA

Valentine. Julia has told him that she loves him, too; they exchange a much more cursory goodbye than the fond parting between Proteus and Valentine, and swap rings.

When Proteus arrives in Milan, he finds that his friend has fallen in love with Silvia, the daughter of the duke. She is clever, witty and beautiful – and Proteus instantly falls in love with her, too, completely forgetting his promises to Julia and also compromising his friendship with Valentine. Why does he want Silvia so much? Just because his friend likes her and he can't handle that? He tells Silvia's dad that she's planning to elope with Valentine, getting his 'friend' exiled. What a cad.

Fortunately, Silvia is a sensible and trustworthy woman who is having none of it. She knows all about Julia and – showing more loyalty to a woman she's never met than Proteus does to his fiancée and best friend – tells him off, calling him a 'perjured, false, disloyal man'. She agrees to give him a portrait of herself just so he'll go away.

Poor Julia witnesses all of this. She's come to Milan disguised as a boy called Sebastian, obviously, to 'prevent / The loose encounters of lascivious men'. Just like when Orsino sends Viola (see page 144) to see Olivia in *Twelfth Night*, the odious Proteus hires 'Sebastian' as a page and tells her to take the ring that Julia gave him to Silvia. Crushing. Julia (as Sebastian) tries

> *I do desire thy worthy company, Upon whose faith and honour I repose.*
>
> **ACT 4, SCENE 3**

> *I am so far from*
> *granting thy request*
> *That I despise thee for*
> *thy wrongful suit,*
> *And by and by intend to*
> *chide myself,*
> *Even for this time I*
> *spend in talking to thee.*
> **ACT 4, SCENE 2**

to point out that the woman who gave him the ring loves him, but he doesn't care.

The scene that follows between Julia and Silvia is one of the most touching in the play. There is a real solidarity between these two women, who don't even know each other, that is very much lacking between Proteus and Valentine. Silvia sees Proteus for what he is and is compassionate to Julia's plight – not realising, of course, that it is Julia who's standing in front of her. Rather than hating her rival, Julia appreciates Silvia's kindness.

Why doesn't Julia just sack off the whole idea of marrying Proteus and instead enjoy her newfound freedom as a page, hitting up some Milanese bars and having a good time? Or at least going back to the comfort of her home for some understandable moping? The truth is that Shakespeare doesn't really unpack this. The true reconciliation is going to be between Proteus and Valentine; it's their love for one another that needs to be sorted out.

Everyone ends up in a wood where Valentine has randomly become the leader of some outlaws – because they think he is 'beautified / With goodly shape' and 'a man of such perfection'. He agreed to the role on the proviso that they 'do no outrages / On silly women'. Absolutely not, they say, affronted.

However, it seems that Valentine's best friend has no such qualms.

Silvia, who has gone to look for Valentine, is captured by the outlaws. Proteus 'rescues' her, though she quite sensibly says that she would have preferred a hungry lion – presumably she would have felt safer. She calls him out for being a terrible friend and Proteus nastily responds, 'In love / Who respects friend?' Shockingly, he says he is going to rape her. Julia is standing right there, still pretending to be Sebastian.

Valentine leaps out of hiding and yells at Proteus, who apologises in five short lines and is instantly forgiven. And not only that – Valentine offers to hand over Silvia. It's gross, shocking stuff. Before Proteus can respond, Julia reveals who she really is and Proteus apparently realises the error of his ways. Valentine joins their hands and Proteus says, 'Bear witness, heaven, I have my wish forever.' Julia simply replies, 'And I mine' – does this sound ominous to anyone else? – while Silvia says . . . nothing at all. For the rest of the play. Her dad turns up and says she can marry Valentine after all, as he has 'deserved her'. She has been in love with him since they met – whether this easy forgiveness of his best bud throws any doubt on that, we don't know.

It's all ickily tied up in Valentine's last lines: '. . . our day of marriage shall be yours, / One feast, one house, one mutual happiness.' It doesn't seem to matter who they are marrying (or how they have behaved); Valentine and Proteus just want to be together. That has been the problem all along.

The Two Gentlemen of Verona is thought to be one of Shakespeare's earliest attempts at comedy. Luckily for all of us, he got much better at it. Here he seems to be trying out ideas that recur in later plays. In Julia and Silvia, we see two spirited young women who deserve much more than the idiots/plot they end up with. Thankfully, their 'descendants' – Rosalind (see page 84), Beatrice (see page 26), even Hermia and Helena (see page 42) – will have a much better time of it.

RSC STAGE HISTORY

In 1970, Robin Phillips cast Helen Mirren as Julia and Estelle Kohler as Silvia in his production of *The Two Gentlemen of Verona* set in a 1960s lido. The cast were students holidaying in Italy and included Patrick Stewart as Lance with Blackie the dog as Crab. 'All You Need Is Love' by The Beatles was among the soundtrack to reflect the 60s vibe.

KATHERINA (KATE)

THE TAMING OF THE SHREW

Ten things we hate about the patriarchy

MY TONGUE WILL TELL THE ANGER OF MY HEART, OR ELSE MY HEART CONCEALING IT WILL BREAK.

ACT 4, SCENE 1

KATHERINA (KATE)

Have you heard the joke about the Hallmark Christmas movies – that it would be better to watch them backwards because then you have a story of a woman who leaves her small-town life and unambitious boyfriend, moves to the big city and gets a great new wardrobe? *The Taming of the Shrew* is like that. If we could reverse the plot, we'd see a meek, abused wife become a fiery, righteously angry lady who is *done* with men and isn't going to take any more of their crap. Sadly, this is not the order in which Shakespeare wrote it. Katherina is a great character, but – depending on how you read it – this can be a difficult play for modern audiences.

The first thing to know about *The Taming of the Shrew* is that it's presented as a play within a play. Shakespeare uses the device of having characters watch or act out a play a lot – think Bottom and his friends in *A Midsummer Night's Dream* (see page 42) or the performance of the Players that Hamlet makes everyone sit through (see page 34). He often draws our attention to the fact that what we are seeing isn't meant to be *real* – it's a representation of life for our entertainment. But the whole of *The Taming of the Shrew* is a performance put on as part of a trick a grand lord is playing on a poor beggar.

A 'shrew' is a bad-tempered, nagging, unfeminine woman. She is a 'funny' stock character that turned up in lots of stories and plays (and still does – think of Sandra Bullock's character in 2009's *The Proposal*). Katherina is the 'shrew' of the title. She is disobedient to her father and rude to everyone. She's also a bit handy with her fists. Her sister, Bianca, on the other

WHEN YOUR FRIEND IS TALKING TO A LOT OF PEOPLE ON THE DATING APPS:

Of all thy suitors here
I charge thee tell
Whom thou lov'st best:
see thou dissemble not.

WHEN YOU'VE RESERVED THE TABLE IN THE PUB BUT ANOTHER GROUP IS SITTING THERE:

Let him that moved you hither
Remove you hence.
I knew you at the first
You were a movable.

WHEN YOU HAVE A COLD AND YOU REALLY WANT SOMEONE TO POP TO THE SHOP FOR YOU:

I prithee go and get me some repast,
I care not what, so it be
wholesome food.

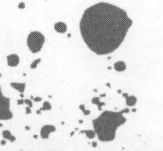

KATHERINA (KATE)

> *If I be waspish, best beware my sting.*
>
> **ACT 2, SCENE 1**

hand, is sweet and compliant (and kind of boring). Everyone wants to marry Bianca. Katherina thinks her dad prefers Bianca, too. Is this why she's so angry? A number of men refer to her as 'Kate the curst' – is this a reputation she's acquired as a result of having her own mind, which has become a bit of a self-fulfilling prophesy? As in, the more she is called angry and aggressive, the angrier and more aggressive she becomes? (Although, she does tie up her sister and hit her at one point, which isn't great.)

The play shows – to us, at least – that there are good reasons why Katherina doesn't want a husband. The men who want to marry Bianca cynically compete for her, and her dad basically auctions her off to the highest bidder. It's all very transactional. Three of the men are wearing a disguise, pretending to be someone else to get close to Bianca. A lot of people are lying about something.

Katherina's dad says Bianca can't get married until Katherina does. Her suitors are up in arms, because who will marry this shrew? But then Petruchio turns up wanting a rich wife and – before he even meets her – says he'll marry Katherina; he doesn't care what she's like. The two have a funny interaction where she insults him amusingly and repeatedly, with Petruchio proving himself at least a match for her wit. 'Come, come, you wasp, i' faith, you are too angry,' he says. 'If I be waspish, best beware my sting,' she retorts.

He tells her dad she's agreed to the marriage and is only pretending to hate him, that he'll pop to buy a suit and marry her in a week. He insists on calling her Kate.

From here on in, Petruchio seems intent on gaslighting her. He deliberately behaves strangely in order to confuse and upset her. He shows up to the wedding late, dressed in 'mad attire', and then behaves weirdly, embarrassing her and putting her on the back foot. Afterwards, he rushes her off to his country house, away from her family. Once there, he stops her sleeping and eating, all the while pretending he's being caring. This is how he intends to 'tame the shrew'. Katherina tries to retain her sense of self – 'Your betters have endured me say my mind, / And if you cannot, best you stop your ears' – but how is she to do this in the face of the barrage of his mad, erratic behaviour? It seems that Petruchio's lines are meant to be funny – in that there are jokes and wordplay – but to modern audiences, at least, it looks very much like controlling, abusive behaviour. Eventually, Katherina gives in. Whether he has broken her down or she has just decided to go along with it, it's hard to say. She agrees with him that the sun is the moon so that he will take her back to Padua for her sister's wedding.

> *I see a woman may be made a fool, If she had not a spirit to resist.*
>
> **ACT 3, SCENE 2**

At the end of the play, Petruchio, Bianca's new husband, Lucentio, and another man who has recently got married make a bet over whose wife is the most obedient. The three women are called to their husbands, but only Katherina complies. Not Bianca, the apparently 'perfect' woman, who tells Lucentio he's an idiot for making a stupid bet. Katherina gives a long speech about how women should obey their husbands – 'thy lord, thy life, thy keeper, / Thy head, thy sovereign'.

So what are we to make of this transformation? Katherina's speech is over the top. She says that a woman owes it to her husband to be obedient because he 'commits his body / To painful labour both by sea and land' for her, while we know that these three privileged dilettantes do nothing of the sort. Has Katherina just learned to play the game, perhaps with Petruchio's encouragement? Or is he simply an abuser who has succeeded in his aim of transforming her from 'a wild Kate to a Kate / Conformable as other household Kates'. A lot rests on their relationship – do we believe she has any affection for him? Is she laughing at his jokes or the victim of them?

The set-up of the story – as a play within a play – tells us that we are not meant to take it seriously. It's not like Shakespeare is writing a hard-hitting domestic drama here. There is a sense that he is satirising the institution of marriage and the expectations men have of women. At the time he was writing, there was a female monarch on the throne, who famously refused to get married (but liked watching plays). Is he implying that there was a lot of wisdom in that decision? That's definitely one reading, but it doesn't make it any easier to find the humour in Petruchio's treatment of Katherina.

Shakespeare never tells us what to think, so we are left with a lot of ambiguities. And as the daughter of a wealthy man, Katherina's only option, realistically, by the standards of the day, is to get married. But does she really need to be *tamed*? While the events of this play seem well out of date, the idea of the woman who won't fit into what men/society expect of her has stuck around – after all, the play inspired the classic 90s romcom *10 Things I Hate About You*. It's hard not to wish that we could have had another scene with the couple after they leave Bianca's wedding feast so we can see what they are like together, alone.

RSC STAGE HISTORY

In 2019, Justin Audibert staged a gender-swapped version of *The Taming of the Shrew* set in a 1590s matriarchal England, with women holding all the power. Katherina was played by Joseph Arkley, and 'Petruchia' by Claire Price. The female costumes, designed by Hannah Clark, were elaborate and ornate Elizabethan gowns that dominated the space, whereas the male actors wore more delicate, subtle attire. The role reversal allowed audiences to look again at the power play between the characters and reconsider the play's problematic ending through fresh eyes.

EMILIA

OTHELLO

Worldly-wise woman does right thing... eventually

LET HUSBANDS KNOW THEIR WIVES HAVE SENSE LIKE THEM: THEY SEE, AND SMELL AND HAVE THEIR PALATES BOTH FOR SWEET AND SOUR, AS HUSBANDS HAVE.

ACT 4, SCENE 3

EMILIA

Complicated, jaded Emilia has some of the best speeches in the whole of *Othello*. In a play that revolves around one man's misplaced sexual jealousy, Emilia gives us a nuanced, even feminist view of why women might cheat. In the context of the early 1600s, when women were meant to be 'virtuous' above anything else, it's incendiary stuff.

Emilia and Desdemona (see page 152) don't know each other when Othello asks Emilia's husband to let her 'attend on' (be a sort of steward to) his new wife. Emilia seems to be older and definitely more experienced in this military world that Desdemona has just stepped into. Desdemona is the daughter of a wealthy senator and, we can assume, of a higher social standing than Emilia. Plus, she is just married and completely in love, whereas Emilia is just trying to get through the day in an abusive relationship with horrible Iago. The two women appear to have little in common.

However, alone in the famous 'Willow Scene', they seem to bond on a deep level, even though they have completely different perspectives on what they are discussing. It's thrilling to watch.

First, there's a lighter moment when they comment on how hot Lodovico, a messenger from Venice who has just turned up, is. 'He speaks well,' ventures Desdemona. 'I know a lady in Venice would have walked barefoot to Palestine for a touch of his nether lip,' says Emilia, far more bluntly. Which makes us want to ask, *Er, are you that lady, Emilia?!* But then the conversation becomes more serious.

Do women really cheat on their husbands? asks Desdemona, as Emilia helps her get ready for bed. *How could they do such a thing?* Emilia says that she might. Not for no reason, but if the circumstances were right. Desdemona says that she absolutely wouldn't.

But men treat women badly, Emilia argues. *And if they hit us, cheat, are jealous for no reason,* 'slack their duties' – presumably stop having sex with their wives – *we are going to resent that*. She says that men cheat because it's fun, they fancy someone and they are weak. And don't women have the same flaws? *If men treat us badly and we then behave badly – well, we're just following their example.* 'I do think it is their husbands' faults / If wives do fall.'

It's a strong argument, delivered with the world-weary savvy of someone who has been through the mill and seen a lot. While Iago fixates on Desdemona's sexuality and Othello gets increasingly hysterical about her fidelity, to Emilia it's a given that women have their own sexual desires. Did Emilia ever sleep with Othello as Iago says? We don't know, but it seems like she has given a lot of thought to why women cheat and how men let them down.

But for all her hard-earned wisdom, the reality is that Emilia is bound to awful Iago and she can't escape. She doesn't know exactly what he's plotting, but she must know what a monster he is.

Emilia's theft of Desdemona's handkerchief is what ultimately leads to Desdemona's death. It's Iago's most effective trick. So why does she do it? She takes the handkerchief in Act 3, before their relationship has developed further. It seems like Iago had been going on about it and, on some level, she does want to please him, or at least get him off her back for a while so he stops insulting her. If Emilia is in self-preservation mode, her capacity to think or care about the consequences for others is reduced.

Emilia is first on the scene when Othello kills Desdemona and she witnesses her last words. She lets Othello have it, all guns blazing, when he tells her that she was unfaithful to him. She seems more shocked than we would expect to hear of Iago's part in the whole mess, but that could be because of her dawning horror as she joins the dots and realises the part she has played. She has no fear of Othello, even as he threatens to kill her: 'O gull, O dolt, / As ignorant as dirt! Thou hast done a deed – / I care not for thy sword – I'll make thee known, / Though I lost twenty lives.'

When Iago arrives, she screams at him and calls him a liar. She says she is leaving him, essentially, and she will not shut up, however much the men try to make her. She's determined to out Iago and defend Desdemona, though she does pay for it with her life. Iago kills her and she dies telling Othello that Desdemona loved him – 'So speaking as I think, alas, I die.' Speaking as you think is a dangerous pastime for a woman.

Poor, complex, long-suffering Emilia. She is a victim of male violence just as Desdemona is. For much of the play, she comes across as cynical and unsentimental, but she shows her strength by giving impassioned speeches in defence of her friend and refusing to relent until the world sees her husband for what he really is.

WHEN YOU DON'T KNOW
WHAT SHE SEES IN HIM:

*What should such a fool
Do with so good a wife?*

WHEN SOMEONE IS SPREADING
NASTY RUMOURS:

*If he say so, may his pernicious soul
Rot half a grain a day! He lies to
th' heart.*

A GENERIC RESPONSE WHEN SOMEONE IS
MAKING A FUSS ABOUT NOTHING:

*I am sorry
For your displeasure,
but all will sure be well.*

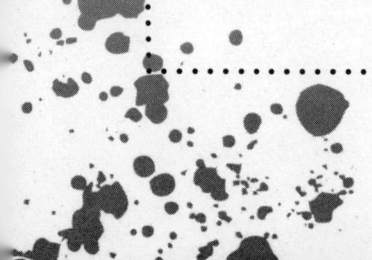

RSC STAGE HISTORY

Ayesha Dharker played a submissive Emilia in Iqbal Khan's 2015 production, which was the first at the RSC to cast a Black actor, Lucian Msamati, as Iago. Msamati's Iago was a charming, lively joker but was also a sadistic manipulator and tormenter of his wife and 'friend'. Emilia and Desdemona's (Joanna Vanderham) strong female friendship shone through in their duet of the 'Willow' song.

Acknowledgements

The RSC would like to thank HarperCollins for commissioning *Shakespeare's Strong Women*, which champions both Shakespeare's famous female characters as well as some lesser-known, but equally intriguing, roles. Specific thanks to Harriet Prideaux for imagining the concept and having the persistence to ensure its publication; Tom Asker for his endless patience and seeing it through to completion; designers Catherine Wood and Poppy Loughtman for beautiful iterations of RSC assets; as well as Sarah Hammond, Holly Kyte, Hetty Touquet and Daniela Mestriner for all their hard work.

Special thanks to Liz Marvin for her humour, wisdom and unique interpretation of Shakespeare's women through words, and to Clementine Hope for bringing the characters to life through striking modern illustrations. Thanks also to Juliet Stevenson, RSC Associate Artist, for her personal foreword.

RSC thanks to Brandgenuity, particularly Aisling Williams for tenacity at the outset, and to Chloe Smith and Jordan Crozier for their support throughout. Gratitude also to Vickie O'Malley at Rockpool Licensing for her expertise.

At the RSC, thanks go to Michelle Morton for managing the project, to Vinota Karunasaagarar and Beckie Rodgers for encouragement and proofreading skills, and to Jacqui O'Hanlon and Rob Hayes for advocating and supporting the publication. With appreciation to all at the RSC for their ongoing assistance of brand licensing collaboration projects.